ALONE

The First Australian Woman to Row the Atlantic Ocean

MICHELLE LEE

Published by Wilkinson Publishing Pty Ltd
ACN 006 042 173
PO Box 24135, Melbourne, VIC 3001, Australia
Ph: +61 3 9654 5446
enquiries@wilkinsonpublishing.com.au
www.wilkinsonpublishing.com.au

Follow Wilkinson Publishing on social media.

 WilkinsonPublishing
 wilkinsonpublishinghouse
 WPBooks

ISBN: 9781922810137
A catalogue record for this book is available from the
National Library of Australia.

Cover and internal design by Jo Hunt.

Printed and bound in Australia by Griffin Press.

CONTENTS

FOREWORD

It isn't often in life that you get to meet someone that has the potential to change the way you look at life! Someone genuinely self sufficient, self motivated and immensely inspiring to those around them. Michelle became this person in my life.

I first met Michelle when she came to me as a patient around 15 years ago. She had obvious skin problems, her hands were red and raw in areas and she had a terrible rash on her body. She was fatigued and quite distraught at what her body was doing. The eczema that had plagued her since childhood had returned with vengeance. Because she worked as a massage therapist it was obvious that she needed immediate relief, and because I worked with many chronically ill patients, and Michelles eczema was a chronic illness, I knew that there was a great need for some deep analytical detective work to get to the bottom of why she suffered with the eczema, so it could be completely cleared. Without finding the 'why' I knew the eczema would be a life-long companion for her.

I saw her weekly and treated her with herbal formulas, homeopathic remedies and diet modifications. She was improving physically week-by-week, but there was a part of her that seemed emotionally spent. So I suggested we do some deeper emotional work, using vibrational energy and acupressure tapping work along with some hypnotherapy and guided visualisations. She desperately wanted to heal so she enthusiastically agreed.

Emotional work can be very challenging. She was wavering with how she could answer the questionnaire that I started patients off with, as it is quite a deep and involved set of questions. As she started to get into it, she had some lightbulb moments, noticing patterns of behaviour and beliefs she held onto that didn't seem to represent who she was now, and as she gained further insight into who she was, how she was expressing her emotions, she began seeing and recognising the deep truth of why she had the eczema. This gave me the starting point to begin unravelling her past and working to bring healing not only to her body but to her emotions and her mental state as well. It was quite a journey.

As each month passed Michelle was finding ways to not only bring balance and harmony into her life but to actually better herself, to challenge herself and to fully trust herself and importantly to trust her body. It was inspiring to watch her grow. It really was like a butterfly emerging from a cocoon.

Somewhere along the line, Michelle found a new lease of life and did her eventful 'alone' holiday to Indonesia where she met Tony, who became her someone that changed the direction of her life. The rest of Michelle's story you can read in this book.

Michelle has written this book from her heart. She lays it all out, the good and the not so good, the ups and the downs.

What started as a patient practitioner relationship has blossomed into a beautiful friendship, for that I will be forever grateful. I know Michelles story, I know her background, her childhood experiences, and yet, as I read the words Michell has written in her book, I was transported there with her. I felt a great surge of joy and a deep respect for her honesty as I read her words.

She has grown into owning who she is, owning her truth and

speaking her truth. She has found her purpose in life, and she bravely steps into it every day. She is certainly one of the most inspirational people I have ever had the great pleasure and honour to know.

She is truly an inspiration, one of a kind, a loyal and loving friend. A gift to humanity.

Molly Knight
Dip. Nutr., Dip. CH., Dip. Irid.,
Grad Dip Herbal Medicine.

CHAPTER 1

DEFINING MYSELF

To be all that you are, and all that ever have been, is all perfect.

To wind up where you are, right now, in your current point in your life is a combination of exactly that. All that you were.

Think of your struggles, trials, tribulations and your wins, triumphs and podium moments.

This is your journey. Mine has not all been smooth coastal sailing with blue bird skies – aka, rainbows and butterflies.

There has been turmoil, upheaval and rage. Home should be a safe haven. It should be the one place you can go, when your world is falling apart around you. Home should make you feel "ahhhh". You know – that sigh of pure relief, when you reach safety. Our home was very rarely that. In fact, my memories are of yelling, arguing, fighting and disharmony.

Padstow Heights, my welcome to the world for my first 5 years. Born to Margaret and Ray Lee.

My sister Kathryn was 6 years old when I was born and she said I had to be named Michelle. So, Michelle Louise Lee I am.

Significant and inspired by my sister's best friend name – at the time. I have no idea of my time of birth. It is these details of my life that were never talked about or – as my friends' do with their kids, rejoice – on their birthdays'.

My brother Anthony is less than a year older than me – 363 days in fact. Born 7 August 1971.

Our mother never shared anything about her childhood openly and our curiosity was unwelcomed, so early on that I now can say that I know very little about her life.

I am aware that her upbringing was tough. Poppy came back from World War 2 damaged – mentally. He was an alcoholic and later died of bowel cancer.

Mum, being the oldest of 6 siblings came with responsibilities just shy of running and maintaining a household – while her mother became the bread winner.

I do remember Mum telling me how she had to make sure her brother and sisters were ready for school each day.

I am sure that my Mum's mental state is a reflection of her past. Her conditioning and beliefs were set amongst tough and hard times. Apparently, she wanted 6 children – and endured 3 miscarriages in the gap between my brother and sister, 5 years.

To understand the turmoil and disharmony in our household explains possibly why I so consciously chose not to have children, or to be a mother.

There was an element of thought "what if I had what my mother had and treated kids the same way?"

Although I am now confident that I do not have the afflictions my mother suffers, I am relieved that I never became a mother. No regrets at all with that choice. It was the right decision.

My sister on the other hand says that she always wanted to be a mother and that she regrets never having the opportunity. I think my sister is similar to Mum – mentally. That statement would be fighting words, of course. She was engaged once, but never married. There was a long story with that. Her fiancé was Danish.

Apparently, they practice witchcraft and my sister is positive that they put a spell on her at some point. Mum hated on Katherine, intensely. For as long as I can ever remember. There was no love shown towards her and the relationship was toxic, at best. Why she was hated so deeply is unknown to me.

Dad was never around to see the abuse mum dished out on Kath. He was gone from dawn til dark. Often my brother and I would be ripping mum off Kath; pretty traumatic at age 4, 5 and 6.

After years of me silently questioning what illness my mother had, I took myself to the family GP, Les Pate, also best mate of my dad.

A character in his own right, Les Pate had witnessed mum's "episodes" – for lack of a better word. He had experienced the wrath of her sharp tongue firsthand.

I decided I would book an appointment to see if Les could shed any light on the situation. He did. He admitted and confirmed that my thoughts of mental illness were present. He asked me what I thought mum had. "schizophrenia?" I replied, "you know – multiple personalities." He said no. Not schizophrenia but definitely a chemical imbalance that could be controlled on prescriptive medication. He said the good thing was that you could achieve a level, sane and logical person on monitored medication.

• • •

Our back yard was one of many pleasures. We rode BMX bikes till the sun went down and rode horses through paddocks and terrain that you could have sworn made you feel like real life cowboys and indians.

My brother would make awesome bike tracks with dad's farm tractor and later, when he could reach the pedals, the bulldozer.

It was action packed on the weekends with a bit of everything happening. I will never forget the time my brother tied Jodie Green by the ankle to Bennie the German Shepherd.

Bennie loved to play fetch with a stick or a ball. Anthony threw the stick as far as he could, Bennie took off with the power of what looked like 6 horses. Jodie's legs got ripped out from under her. She screamed as Bennie dragged her along the ground – she crossed a multitude of surfaces – gravel, grass and dirt. He then returned as diligently as ever, giving poor screaming Jodie another dose of torture.

My brother copped the biggest hiding from dad that night. Mum screamed "You bastard Anthony, wait till your father gets home!" Well, you can guess how that ended. Jodie never saw the funny side to that but did question why she let him tie her ankle to the dog in the first place.

Garren McCalla – my brother's mate, was there. I think he was pretty traumatised by the whole scene. There were many instances that occurred where I am sure most people would be horrified. My brother was on first name terms with the emergency staff at Camden Hospital. His visits included multiple concussions – usually from football but also from falls off his horse "Red". He even rolled a ride on lawn mower once – he was curious what sort of angle it could maintain.

Never dull, never just quiet and mundane with Anthony. I love and hate that. To be anything but is boring. It is safe. It lacks excitement.

Our afternoons were always spent in the pool in summer. I remember the summers being particularly hot. There were even some days at school when they "call it off". They would actually call school over and closed for the day, send us kids home! We always ended up with school mates over. The pool would be full of kids.

Other times in the extreme heat, teachers would have everyone lay on the floor with the overhead fans on and the lights off. I used to love that. The whirring of the fans and dimly lit room with our teacher watching over us like the shepherd over her lambs. Those memories are nice to recall. It was the harmony I lacked in the home. It was a yearning that I didn't know existed – until I experienced it.

• • •

Pivotal moments in my childhood were the ones where I would be in deep trouble. I learned very young that lying only got you in more trouble; running and hiding was never an option.

I tried to run away several times. Taking my hard case - burnt orange school bag - I carefully put my PJs, buffy (my white empty bodied, stuffing-less pussy cat) and my pencils inside, shut the lid and snapped the locks down. I was leaving home.

I had nowhere to go and I was scared. The sun was going down rapidly. I knew I didn't have long to get to my undesignated place. For what wrongdoing I do not remember but, I copped a hiding with dad's belt. He cracked it across my arse and thighs hard enough to leave welts and a burning sensation that left before the welts did.

It was on the path between the clothesline and the outside toilet. I remember him being outraged by my crime. With that, I packed my bag.

My sister came with me. She took me to the horse float which was acting as a nursery to a little piglet. His mother was shot by a farmer and the bullet ricocheted off her. It hit the little piglet and damaged his front leg. We got him and nursed him. He grew up to be like a puppy dog – following us wherever we went. At this time however, he was occupying the horse float. We sat on the floor with him and I wondered how long we would stay here before we moved on. Like, actually left home.

My sister comforted me and I soon forgot about the hiding. My hunger took on too much priority. Then, just as though she mind-read me, Mum called "Kathryn. Michelle. Dinner is ready" What?. Could she read my mind? It was dark now – and cold. The piglet loved having us in his company. I now wondered how long we could hide out for without starving to death. I forgot to put any food in my bag.

It wasn't long before we dragged our tail between our legs, head bowed and entered through the back sliding door. Mum put our dinner on the table without saying a word. My sister and I ate in silence, me touching her leg the whole time for comfort.

She really did protect me. I went to her for everything. I used to wet the bed till I was about 5. In the middle of the night, I never once thought of waking Mum. I would go across to my sister and she would silently take me to the bathroom, run the bath, add alpha Kerri oil to the warm water and rinse my poor red, inflamed and sore skin. Then she would take me back to her bed.

It served a purpose. You see, it meant that I would then get to sleep with my sister. She was just 9 and I was 3.

Those memories are vivid, strong and firm in my mind. I can see the whole scene as though I am hovering above, looking down.

Just to write about and recount it in the full detail stings my heart. It is with warm tears running down my face that I recall these moments. It is as though it has awakened the little girl in me. The scared, nervous, anxious and want to be hugged little girl. The one who wants to believe in rainbows and butterflies. The memories. There is a deep sadness that evokes a need to protect and preserve the corners of your heart to dampen the need to burst into tears.

CHAPTER 2

SIBLINGS

My brother Anthony - Dickie, Dick, Annie and Tony, to his mates – and I would talk and chitter chatter for hours in the back of the car on those revolting, never ending long drives that we endured as kids.

Dad would drive to Dubbo or Queensland with zero breaks. You would be begging to stop to go to the toilet and he would finally pull over for you to squat behind a tree, on the roadside, somewhere in the middle of nowhere.

Why Dubbo or Queensland? Well, Dubbo was where Uncle Barry and Aunty Judy lived on thousands of acres. They always made sure that we had a potty calf, lambs or piglets to bottle feed at the crack of dawn during our visits. They would let us drive tractors and even taught me how to drive a manual. We loved visiting them.

They were childless. Unable to have children of their own, they certainly took advantage of treating us like one of their own. School holidays were often spent in their custody. Aunty Judy just loved having us and spoilt us with love and attention. The 6-hour drive there with maniac Ray at the wheel and whinging Margaret was character building, unavoidable torture we all had to endure.

When we got a bit older, we were sent on a plane, by ourselves and were greeted by Judy and Barry at the airport. That was a warmly received luxury from about age 7.

The car trips were back in the day when you could climb over the back seat and lay down in your station wagon. I would explain to my brother how the rear demister worked on the back wind screen; how the heat would travel along the wire inserted into or stuck on to the glass and it would melt away the fog. For some reason this story never got tiresome.

We would do the 12 + hour drive up to sunny Queensland to visit Big Nan – Mum's mum. She lived on the Gold Coast and these visits were my least liked. They were guaranteed to have a tone of hostility at some point.

For whatever reason, my mum and her mother did not get on. They always had a "I hate you" match with each other. You never knew what started or created the spark for the uncomfortable and viscous outcome. It was like steam in a kettle – slow to build then scrrreeeaaaammmmmm, they would.

To this very day my brother, sister and I do not know the nature of the relationship my mum and nan had. You could work out that there was resentment and even hatred between them. It was both ugly and unpleasant.

Anthony grew up idolising dad. He wanted to be just like him – he just was I guess. He did follow him and was encouraged to play with anything remotely mechanical. He had every Lego set and tool kit you could think of as a toddler.

Then, one day, in the silence and absence of Anthony, Mum went looking to see what he was doing. Oh shit. He proudly explained, "Yep, I've filled all the cars up". He had run the garden hose into the tanks of the family car and the Toyota 4WD.

You can imagine how that went down at the dinner table that night. Mum was scared to tell Dad. The outburst that followed was of yelling, ranting, raving and a sense of exasperating bewilderment.

My bro just said, "I was only trying to help". What could you say to that? He was mimicking and mocking Dad from as early as you can. He was driving machinery as soon as he could reach the pedals. Who wouldn't want to play on tractors and push dirt around with bulldozers?

Anthony did work with Dad for a number of years. It was feisty at times with a battle of 2 very strong wills and personalities; a case of being young and open to doing things differently versus tried, tested and can't teach an old dog new tricks.

My brother could build anything with metal. Welding became his passion and specialty.

Today he is respected and highly regarded in the mining industry for his workmanship and work ethics. Delivering over and above expectations is what he does naturally – which has earned him job security wherever he goes.

This was a trait passed down from our dad. If you could bottle up someone's great traits and own them as your own, which would you choose?

My brother has loyalty, honesty, logic and practicality at his core. On top of that he has a work ethic greater than most and can hold his head high in his capabilities. I am so proud of my brother.

During the Covid pandemic, he put integrity first and came out trumps. In his efforts to reject the fucking mandates workplaces were pushing (no jab no job) Anthony found another job to avoid the poisonous clot shot.

He went to work for a small family business in town, taking a significant pay cut. After 2 days of seeing how they carried out their business, Anthony decided it was not for him.

He walked into the boss's office and politely and respectfully told him this was not how he operated and that the work being done was not of the service and quality he was happy to put his name to.

With that, the boss asked him how he thought it should be done. Anthony explained what he would do if it were his business and, boom, the boss said, "Stay – do it your way, the correct way!" Wow. There you go. Integrity from one encourages and promotes the same from some one else.

This is the law of attraction in perfect action. My brother's attitude changed that of the manager. He could have said, "take a hike" but, I believe that the way my brother approached it sparked and ignited a desire to be better.

We can all do this. Know that like attracts like and be brave enough to speak our truth.

I had many years of disconnect with my brother, years that I will never get back. It was over an incident with my sister and an expectation that she proposed to myself and then husband, Shane.

When my brother expressed his distaste in her request to us, he told her so in no uncertain terms. This then made me get mad at him and as a result we did not speak for many years.

Now, although in regular contact, we still have not spent much time together as he lives in far North Queensland and I live in Sydney.

I looked up to my bro growing up and admire his capabilities now. At school, in the year below him, I was known as the 'reserve bank'. Come Wednesday or Thursday Anthony would find me in the schoolground at lunch or recess and hit me up for some dough.

We each received an allowance of 10 bucks each on a Monday. It was up to us to budget that money week to week. If you played an away sport, the budget would feel the pinch as it was an extra expense. So, I often did a sport that stayed at school, allowing my $$$ to last longer, or, help my bro out. I never protested and didn't mind giving him a top up. It was never on a 'to be repaid' basis. It was just a given. He would do the same for me now. And I for him. I like that. There is no tit for tat.

At now age 50, he has mellowed somewhat. He was balding by

age 25 and bald by 30. He can turn his hand to anything and is more like Dad than he probably even knows. I like this, too.

. . .

La (real name Kathryn), my sister, is shorter than me, 6 years my senior, dark haired, blue eyes and sharp as a tack. She's articulate and not afraid of confrontation.

We are polar opposites. While I will avoid conflict, La tends to thrive in it. She has represented herself at court in cases against big corporations and once was even mistaken as "the solicitor for the defendant".

Growing up she was the best big sister you could wish for. I went to her for everything. La would comfort and console me through my infant years at Leppington Public school.

For whatever reason I would be crying and sobbing uncontrollably and the teacher, Mrs Perry, would carry me on her hip to my sister, pullingl her out of class to settle me.

We would often leave home to go to school after some kind of wild turmoil the night before. Mum and Dad would have a screeching match and argue into the night. I remember my nerves being shattered and my stomach feeling like it had a knot inside it. I am certain this was the reason for my crying. I'd cling to my sister while she told me to "shhhh, everything will be ok" There was no more words than that. Not that I can recall.

Eventually, exhausted, I would stop and pull myself together. Mrs Perry would take me back to join my class.

Kath was abused mentally, physically and verbally by our mother. I don't know why she hated her so much.

Why, at 5am would she be pulling my sister out of bed, by the hair of the head. What did she do to deserve that? Nothing. I can't even explain it to this day.

Mum would be yelling at her, La would be screaming. My

brother would physically reef my mum's grip from my sister.

Somehow, we had to function normally, get ourselves to school and try to pretend that it never happened. You dared not share this shit with your friends. What would they think of you?

This is why I was so sensitive to tone for years into my adult life, even now.

We, all 3 of us were, affected in different lasting ways. I am sure this is why we are not married with children. I know for one thing, I feared that if I did become a parent, what if history repeated itself and I became a version of our mother?

My sister was put down by Mum. She would bag her out. She would physically abuse her. To write this causes great sadness and heaviness in my heart. It is not something I talk about much, as it creates pain and digs up emotions laid to rest. I can't even say that this has been resolved.

The dislike between my Mum and sister is still alive. Whilst it is impossible for me to hold any anger abouts the situation now, I can understand that my sister would feel strongly against our mother.

My saving grace was that I left the family home aged 18. I moved out with 2 girlfriends, and never went back. Exiting from the disharmony so young was definitely better for my mental and nervous health.

I can talk about it but thinking about it is a whole other story. I did a lot of work emotionally during 2011 to 2016 in relation to the deep sadness I would feel and the guilt I would experience when good things came my way.

It was difficult to accept wins in life without feeling intense guilt and undeserved feelings. I particularly noticed it as a problem while with Tony. I couldn't accept the fact that I did not have to work. It provoked and triggered feelings lacking self-worth.

I really did not feel worthy of an easy or fully supported existence. This is when I realised I disliked owning the debilitating emotion that could easily sabotage me every time.

To say that our childhood was complex is an understatement. We had to learn to function in a less than nurturing and loving environment. To sum it up – I think the 3 of us are incredibly sad when we pay it too much attention. I have learnt to put it a space that is now controlled and will only occasionally rear it's presence.

I still get upset at certain tones spoken between 2 people that may be having a fight I can also feel sad when I see the behaviour in other circles. I wish that no one else would ever have to see, hear or feel it.

Anyway, we are not alone in the family dysfunction. There are plenty of other Aussie families that operated similar to ours, back in the day. Today, kids know their rights and would threaten to call the Department of Community Services on to their parents.

Our escape was weekends. Kathryn would pack the lunch and we would be off, into the bush, on the horses and bikes, swimming in the watercourse and creating our own safe haven and peace from any adult-created turmoil.

These days, my sister carries the scars of the trauma of childhood, I am sure. She has had plenty of ru- ins with individuals in her professional field and personal life. She will not be walked over or taken advantage of and knows how to stick up for herself, which I do like.

Although, perhaps she needs a lesson on delivery in order to prevent rubbing people up the wrong way.

• • •

When was this? I had a yearning for change: Recognition that my current baggage was no longer serving me; that the little girl needing a hug only gave rise to victim status.

I began a path of trying something new. Inspired and instigated by one of my massage clients, Colleen.

She was a natural therapy guru, having consulted with her naturopath for several years. Colleen introduced me to Ludmilla, a Russian/Chinese naturopath who had a lifetime of experience and knowledge.

Ludmilla came into my life at my lowest point, health-wise. I looked like a burns victim with red, itchy, angry and sore skin. The worse it had ever been. At the same time, I was going through an emotional, internal turmoil. Internal because I never shared it with anyone.

It was when I had thoughts of leaving husband? Shane for a life I imagined - one that I would look at the glass and see it as half full.

My time with Shane was calm, harmonious and beautiful. But it was lonely. We both worked opposite each other for a lot of our relationship. The club industry was Shane's full-time employment and he worked at 2 different clubs, much to my insistence.

I was obsessed with the idea of owning our property and being debt free by 40. We both maintained 60 hours every week and both had 2 jobs. I worked fulltime in the State Bank and then weekends at Parramatta Leagues club while Shane worked at Parra Leagues and Parra RSL.

It was anti-social and not counter intuitive for restoring a failing marriage – largely due to loneliness and the drift of separation that shift work adds – like a wedge that is tightly driven between 2 objects intentionally to create separation.

I had a strong desire to not own this crap anymore.

CHAPTER 3

KICK IN THE GUTS

On the day of my departure maybe put date in here to the start line for the race across the Atlantic, my brother phoned at 8am. "Dad is going in for emergency surgery, the doctors are not holding a lot of hope".

Wow. Kick me in the guts once. Then, ready or not for that second, unexpected kick to the guts. 11am – "Are you sitting down? He didn't make it!" So final were his words.

I was lucky enough that my brother put the phone to Dad's ear pre surgery, while he still fully conscious, lucid and aware. I did get that opportunity to say I will come and visit you as soon as this ocean is rowed. I did get to say "I love you Dad".

I was due to board my flight at 4.40pm that day. My world and pain and grief for all that could never be now hit me like a sledge hammer.

As I sat on the top stair at home gripping Karen's arm – my roomie, I realised just how stubborn I had been all these years and that my regret in life would last for the term of my own remaining life. As if he were in the room, I heard him say "Don't you dare stand over a hole in the ground, crying over me – you go and row that ocean." A value I hold so strong, he was somebody who did what he loved and loved what he did.

I thank him for the values that I also hold so strong, in work ethic and conviction in my beliefs, without too much care for what "people think".

I wrote this eulogy during my flight, for my sister to read in my absence on my behalf.

In his legacy, I decided to still go and row that ocean. My row became my appreciation to all that he taught me, through tough love, lead by example and by the only way he knew to teach me. It wasn't perfect in delivery and yes, I could think of many ways it could've been done better but, it was his way and ultimately, I am more like him than I possibly like.

"Dad - Raymond – Ray.

How do you sum up the life that was of someone who had been so long absent in your own? For reasons that now all seem so insignificant.

He's life cut short abruptly and grossly contradictory to how he chose to live, is unfair to say at best.

From early memories, Dad was a devoted, motivated, driven, passionate, honest and hard-working quintessential Fair Dinkum typical Aussie bloke. In his signature Akubra hat, R & M Williams moleskins and Boots, he would leave the house in the dark and not return, till the dark.

He was a workaholic.

He loved what he did and did what he loved.

He worked hard and played hard. Dad exuded an enthusiasm for life, a love for horse riding, he was highly respected and skilled at the art of moving dirt. He was good at whatever he chose to turn his hand at. This is a trait and Legacy he has passed down to Anthony, our brother, who would go to work with Dad and drive tractors, grease and oil change machinery and in later years, step up to the challenge of trying to " teach an old dog new tricks"... not always ending so well.

He had a few sayings that I can vividly heard. he was a believer of "you do the crime – you do the time " and if you erred – aka, fucked up, he would say "oh well, you made your bed now lie in it!"

Sick days were forbidden, sleep-ins were unheard of and credit cards unfathomable" in the Lee household. "If you can't pay for it, you are living above your means", Dad would say.

Amongst friends and peers, you couldn't help notice how infectious Dad's personality was. He was the life of the party. He was generous and many bonds were forged over a scotch and Coke – which became iconic in his life.

My ability to call a spade a spade, stand up for myself, live by my own convictions and sense of adventure, are a result of an inherited gene passed on to me – by my dad.

I am grateful for my own work ethic, strength and stamina, which I see as a mirror image of my dad - developed early on, as a result of being a "product of your environment".

Growing up in the Lee household was not always easy but it has given me the tools in life for resilience, independence and a sense of stubbornness that has allowed me to dare to take on the Atlantic Ocean, in a rowing boat. Solo Alone.

I will dedicate this voyage to my dad – in appreciation and gratitude for your life teachings that have all led me to this particular point in my life.

Whilst it wasn't always easy, it has provided me the foundations built on determination, grit and integrity. My row and challenge ahead will expose some dark moments, I am sure.

It'll be in these moments that I will talk to him and ask for all his strength to get me through the storm, until the sun comes out to shine again...

To my family – Mum, Katherine and Anthony – I am sorry I am not there with you to bear the burden of the farewell to our dad, but rest assured, I will raise a glass with a shot of his favourite and take a moment to reflect on the life that was.

Ray, or Raymond when he was in trouble - I'm so sad that your life and chapter ended like it did. I'm grateful that your last breath was taken with your hand in Anthony's and most of all, that you were not alone.

I know I will hold my own regrets and as you would say "oh well, you made your bed now lay in it".

Thank you to everyone who showed up to celebrate our dad's hard-working life. celebrate and grieve. Support each other. Respect each other. Show dignity.

For anyone who has benefited from my dad's generosity and if you have any of his belongings, return them and do what is right. For the low life hangers o's, exit quietly and stay away. Show respect.

Thank you. Michelle. In arms - with my brother and sister."

And that, to say goodbye, was the start of my grieving process.

My week at the starting line pre-race departure, was at best, a blur. I would find myself in and out of waves of chest-aching grief that would wash over me at random and unexpected times and then mostly, fall asleep crying silently about my selfishness, my guilt – of not being there with my brother and sister.

For a brief moment I had to consider withdrawing from the Atlantic Challenge for 2018. My reasons would have been purely out of a sense of obligation to be at the funeral and for standing beside my brother and sister.

My decision to go did conjure up feelings of guilt, selfishness and resentment. I would've resented missing out – blame that on Dad's shitty timing, even though it was out of his hands. Logically I knew that He did not plan this – this way, this time.

My guilt of knowing that my siblings were left to deal with the shit-show that was to inevitably unfold – and did - also highlighted that selfish trait Ray exhibited in his determination to "do what Ray wanted to do".

I didn't have long to decide as my flight was at 2.30pm that afternoon. Evidently, I chose to go. The voice of my dad saying "Don't stand over a hole in the ground crying about me – go. Row that bloody ocean!" So, I did.

CHAPTER 4

MY WHY

There were many times where I questioned the why and how I would do this.

I had that little birdie on my shoulder and I had to fight it constantly.

That was part of my journey and it became very familiar but I also became very good at putting that birdie to sleep - or at least quietening him.

My why was borne out of the desire to 'not die wondering' after obsessing over the possibility for almost 2 years, thanks to a book called "Rowing the Atlantic", by Roz Savage.

I finally admitted that it was crazy but that I simply had to row the Atlantic Ocean.

The craziness dissipated when I truly absorbed that Roz Savage was nobody special and it really opened my eyes to the mere fact that we just have to want something with enough conviction.

That was the day I made the decision and that decision was in May 2016.

It began with a phone call to my bestie – AKA, as "wifey". I explained to her that I wanted to row across the Atlantic Ocean.

She gave me a very cheerful "really honey, how you gonna do

that?" My response was simply "I dunno - I just gotta get me a boat!"

It's that simple! well at least I thought it was going to be that simple. Of course, it was not. It then led me down a path of googling "ocean rowing boats for sale".

It wasn't long before I realised that there were actually none for sale in Australia. So, my mind then thought "you need to speak to somebody who has been there and done that - can't be too hard can it?" Next thing I googled "Australian's Atlantic Ocean row". Only one name came up, it was Andrew Abrahams on the Gold Coast so of course, thanks to social media, I was able to message him immediately:

> **Hi Andrew. I want to do the Atlantic Ocean row. Where to start, how to attract sponsers, how best to train, where to get my little, row boat, how to become a part of this phenomenal adventure? Making it happen. Your ideas, knowledge, know how and advice would be so greatly appreciated. Many thanks, Michelle. Castle Hill, Sydney, Australia**

He shot back a response almost immediately "happy to help. Email or call me".

So, I picked up the phone. No hello, how are you or small talk BS – straight into the business of "Where in the hell am I gonna get me a boat?" and he laughed and said, "Oh right, are you a rower?" "Oh shit," I thought in that instance. "No, I have never rowed in my life."

A small pause and then he said, "Oh, it's not that important anyway. You need to learn to row in the surf, not on those fancy, long, skinny, light, fast boats!"

My phone call ended with me feeling completely and utterly deflated.

He said people would let you down, they would promise the

world and under deliver, that I would need a year or maybe 2 to prepare and that I would have to build a boat.

That was all pretty danming and then the biggest thing he said that made it sound impossible was "and you will need $200,000". "Well shit! What a negative prick", I thought.

After hanging up, head low, heart heavy, I had a light-bulb moment. "You have done it, other people make it happen, what the hell have you got that, that I don't?". That was it. I picked up the phone, hit redial and awaited his answer.

"You are not the only one in the world that has done this. People do it every year. If you can't help me that is fine but don't you dare, make it sound impossible." Pause. "HMMMMM, so, you are serious then?"

It was as though I had to pass a test to show my determination and intention was real to row an ocean. Well, that was just the beginning of the test I had to pass to prove my intention.

I honestly thought it would be as easy as buying a second-hand boat rowing at a few times in Sydney harbour. shipping that thing to the start line and then rowing the ocean.

What I didn't know was my next 2 years were going to require life changing habits.

I had to learn to row. I had to also build credibility, validation and a profile in order to attract sponsors. To do this, Andrew suggested that I should at the very least commit to the world record and become the fastest female to row one million metres on a Concept 2 indoor rowing machine.

You see, it would tick a lot of boxes; it would a give me the skills to learn to row and master the technique of rowing in addition it would also help my body go through the physiological adaptations of long-distance stamina requires.

It would also be building my mental resilience and then it would give me a title, so that at least when I went knocking on sponsors doors and they asked, "well who are you?", I could now say "I am the world record holder of the one-million-meter rowing challenge".

It all sounded pretty impressive but also very daunting so I asked him what would my life look like if I committed to the world record. He explained that my whole activity would have to revolve around rowing. It would be gruelling with 13 sessions per week where I would row in either the AM of the PM and then opposite my row, I would be doing a strength and mobility program purely based on the rowing movement pattern.

So, after a few months of chatting with Andrew I finally said yes!

Actually, my yes was a lot easier than that because I saw sense and method in the madness.

In September my rowing machine arrived brand spanking new in the box.

I had John – one of my remedial massage clients – over at the time so he stayed while we put it together.

He witnessed excitement of what was about to unfold. Andrew was booked on a flight to come down the following weekend to give me some coaching sessions. He had asked me previously in the months leading up to September to send him some footage of me actually rowing on a rowing machine and his reaction was "Oh dear, you need some help" which came as a bit of a shock to me because I actually thought I was quite a good rower.

I knew I had an above average baseline of fitness – thanks to the crew that I trained with at YV2 explain. I thought that he would be really impressed. But his reaction knocked my confidence.

After completing my 2km time trial, my program was presented via an excel spreadsheet.

Whilst the numbers seemed really daunting, the schedule was completely overwhelming. I had to give up everything that I loved at the time I was doing cycling climbing I was doing the hanging on the lira silks and trapeze class, did cross-fit style training Monday to Saturday and I had an awesome and varied training schedule full of activities that I absolutely loved and that were my highlight of my every day. All this had to change.

I had to give it all up so that I could just focus on rowing and mastering the technique as well as allowing my body to adapt physiologically to long distance stamina and endurance.

So, every single Sunday I would roll in that machine for 8 whole hours Every Monday I did a 6 hour session and then every other day I had an undulating program that included sprints and just-easy taken over long distance numbers during my 8 hour rows.

Every single Sunday my bestie Claudie would come over to entertain me and keep me fed and fuelled to boost my morale - and supply me with stories of her online dating escapades.

In the whole 6 months there was only 2 Sundays she did not sit by me. Her support was completely unwavering and all during this Claudine was going through her own turmoil and recovery from losing her husband, Tiny, suddenly. He was so named because he was huge in body and huge in soul and personality.

He had a massive fatal heart attack at work function with his workmates, beer in hand. The news was delivered by policemen knocking on her door and asking if she is the wife of David O'Keefe. They delivered the news in the manner in which they are taught - without emotion, just very matter of fact.

My training regime was approached with diligence, discipline and enthusiasm. My body became accustomed to the arduous and long hours.

My mental resilience was definitely being developed as I rowed without stimulus of TV, which was a conscious choice. I'd lived without TV since 2012 when my husband Shane and I finally parted ways after 22 years of togetherness. I took that opportunity to rid my space of TV. It served no purpose or joy for me so it made sense not to own one ever again. I have zero curiosity for what is happening in the news. I have no time to just sit and watch sitcoms for kicks. I have no inclination to lounge and in fact watching people lounge is very irritating to me.

My flatmate often laughs if I do ever sit on the lounge she says, "Michelle you look like you are just waiting for a bus. Sit back and relax", but that idea is completely foreign to me and I have no desire to do so.

During those long rows I would listen to carefully selected podcasts that provided learning and education – usually around health and fitness.

I loved the tapping techniques that were presented by Nick Ortner, an American with the techniques from the Tapping Solution Podcast.

I was also heavily influenced by Martin Rooney from TFW. He produces an amazing Podcast called "Into the Roar". I love the local boys Lachy and Ralph from "The Mind Muscle Project".

They all came across the Atlantic with me and I continued to listen to their material over and over again.

There were times however, when I just needed pure silence.

My neighbour Colin – in his eighties - would often come and sit with me on a Sunday morning after his church service and sometimes he would go over the sermon with me. He would often realise when I've had enough. He'd ask "would you prefer I just sit with you in silence?" and I would just nod gratefully. He obviously was quite intuitive to read that I had had enough "godliness" in that session.

Colin (Stoner) was a man in a loveless marriage and was almost ready to go into that slow downward spiral of decline, when you surrender to the "I'm getting old" tune.

I like to believe that my row and adventure hauled him out of it and gave him a new lease on life, for he was always on the ready when I had tow my boat, launch, retrieve, pick up parts. He rode shotgun next to me, was full-on moral support and my number 1 supporter.

CHAPTER 5

METHOD OF THE MADNESS

I followed my training program religiously, diligently and without too much complaint. My focus was on that world record.

I put a couple of extra pressures on myself personally. For example, I said "if I can't achieve this world record in beautifully controlled environment - with the support and nutrition, air con, ice baths and all of those creature comforts - then I would not be allowed to go and row across an ocean."

With that in mind, I paid extra attention to my sleep and recovery - which you were always in deficit - and that is the specific and intended design of the program; to keep the body in a state of "not quite enough recovery" – again, all adding to my resilience building for the real event.

Part of my recovery strategy was to have a regular fortnightly osteo appointment in order to keep anything niggling at bay, before it could become sinister.

Although I did find that the rehab side of the program based on mobility all around the moving or rowing fashion kept me super supple and mobile like never before, there were many pluses that came from doing that world record.

My nutrition was complemented by consulting a sports nutritionist. She nailed it. After completing 6 weeks' worth of excel spreadsheet updates after every single rowing session, a report was calculated based on the figures I entered into the programme. It spat out some numbers which basically gave my requirements based on my output every single hour I was performing that task, over 14 hours.

The conclusion was that I had to have 45 g of carbs every hour and then at every 3 hours I needed a full 1000 calorie meal I had to consume 450 mls of liquid for hydration. However, for every degree above 22 in outside temperature I had to add 100 mls.

This science-based approach proved to be absolutely perfect and I followed that so every single Saturday night I would spend my evening prepping for 6am the next day. The night before my 8- and 6-hour long rows, I would make up 8 little piles of 45 g easy digestible, high carbohydrate foods.

At the same time I was learning what worked and what didn't. I learned that Apple was not a good food choice during those long rows as it was too fibrous and the digestive system had to work too hard to deal with it.

Pear was OK and bread was a big no-no. I loved having Turkish delight, dates, rice cream from the tin and when you started to struggle actually eating food, I would resort to glucose aid, out of the bottle! It was awesome for achieving the carbohydrate value without what the bulk food would add to your stomach. When you think of rowing, you are crunching up at the catch phase of the stroke: knees are squished basically up to the chest, so it gets uncomfortable if you've got too much bulk in your stomach to digest.

The experience was very valuable as I took all of those lessons with me across the Atlantic.

Of course, I learned the importance of maintaining calories in the body while you are burning constantly.

I knew first-hand what "hitting the wall" actually meant, when you go into calorie deficit and you have to keep performing. You see a massive decline in performance and it gets to the point where you feel like you have, literally, hit a wall. You just cannot pull another stroke.

I tested all of this so that the method to the madness was even clearer.

I find that when I have a super clear objective, to understand method to the madness makes applying that prescription much easier.

It makes more sense and when you I really could not bother today, I would remind myself of that method to the madness and bingo! I would get my ass out there to that fucking machine and ensure I finished that set.

Rowing for that number of hours and sending the body into states of fatigue and exhaustion does something to the mind. I had plenty of documents where my memory would for some reason recall painful moments of my life of growing up in the Lee household and I would re-live them so vividly - memories that I'd put to sleep for my life basically.

Certainly since my twenties I've tried very hard to close the door on the pain of the memories of my childhood so it seems strange to me that while I'm in pain I would recall even more pain. To this day I still don't understand that but it would go through my head - the sadness that remained from watching my Mum and Dad's abusive relationship and the ripple effect of the sadness watching my Mum cry silently.

I would lay next to her in her bed and would be wiping tears away using her sheet and saying please don't cry mummy. I had no idea why she was crying. Looking back now though I can see the loveless situation that she was in and the turmoil of the condition that my father created with his drinking and yahoo-ing with his cronies (AKA friends). It was all quite ugly and stressful and I remember always feeling like I had a knot in my stomach or an elephant sitting on my chest or 2 fists in my throat.

Later in life I realised the impact of the constant high alert of my nervous system and began to understand the damage stress puts on the body. Stress and nerves or anxiety manifest in the body and will appear as a chronic condition. My condition was severe dermatitis and eczema.

Growing up I would be wrapped in plastic and bandages. Each night mum would stand me on the kitchen table while she wrapped my limbs in a greasy thick ointment. She would liberally apply the transparent ointment to the cling wrap then apply it on my body, securing it all with torn cotton sheets. I would sleep like that every night. My skin was red, inflamed, angry looking and bloody sore.

As the biggest organ of the body, the skin has a significant impact on most things you do. The long-term effects of cortisone use showed up when I changed career.

I went from the corporate world to become a remedial massage therapist. The constant friction of massage broke my thinned skin – a side effect of cortisone use (abuse as it were, in my case).

This is when I decided to take on a new approach. My life changed forever, thanks to my naturopath Ludmilla Mallaroy. She explained that for every year of abuse of cortisone to expect 1 month to heal the damage.

So, in effect, I was looking at a 3-year turn around. My commitment to finding true inner health was motivated by the desire to be pain free and to have normal skin that didn't look ugly with excessive bits flaking everywhere and bleeding open cracks that hurt with every motion my hand made.

Long story short – my lack of peace, joy and harmony in the home attributed to the chronic skin condition.

You can change all of that with persistence, desire and belief.

I decided that I no longer wanted to own the crap from my past, stuff that I had no say in. Stuff that we (my brother and sister) were subjected to simply because we were born into it.

The level of unawareness of our parents astounds me today as I watch my own friends' parent their children.

Anyway, it was that upbringing that gave me the resilience and independence I own today. It actually laid down foundations to last through life's challenges to date. I am grateful. I can see the benefits and accept that it wasn't fun at the time but I came through and am now strong, independent and resilient. So, thanks Mum and Dad, you gifted me that.

CHAPTER 6

MY INNER CIRCLE

People come and go. When you reflect on your life you will recognise that nothing is forever. When it comes to people, we each serve a purpose to another.

Sometimes it is mutual and other times it is simply for your own benefit.

My inner circle is small, none of them being my school-made friends. That was another lifetime ago.

Some friendships go back to Parra Leagues days, when I was 18 and then there are my more recent friends of the last 15 years.

I do not make friends easily. I have a philosophy that I do not have time to have any more friends than I do. My pot of time would not leave enough room for me and it would compromise the time I have for my friends.

Me time is a priority. Apparently, it is because I am an introvert on the Briggs and Myers scale of personality testing. It is the opposite is true, for the extrovert – the personality type recharges when in company with others. I need the alone time to energise.

I suggest taking the test – it is fascinating how much is right on point. If you answer the questions true, you will be blown away at how accurate the description of your personality and traits are. You will also gain an understanding of why you do what you do.

My life has an inner circle which has consisted of the same people for more than 15 years. Then you meet acquaintances through circumstances or work who will remain in your life in that period only. Some will become extended friends with whom you catch up from time to time.

I love how my adventure journey has widened my circle and created a network. The universe or source energy has presented different people in my life at just the right moment to serve a very specific purpose.

• • •

Meet Claudine. We first met back in 2009. I wanted to rent a space with minimal obligation to sign a lease to run my remedial massage business.

Claudine owned a beauty therapy saloon just one street down the road. One afternoon I randomly I entered her saloon and asked if she would be interested in subletting a room to me – as a trial at first and then something long term, if it worked out.

She was warm and friendly and I felt as though I had known her in my life before. She had a familiar sense to me, though I had never met her before ever. She asked "would you like a cuppa?"

Wow. This was at a time when I was struggling with my health due to severe dermatitis and eczema.

I did look like a burns victim. Red, hot and angry skin up my arms, my torso, oozing out of any neckline and broken, bleeding skin on my hands. I was seeing a naturopath and on a journey of self-healing.

Claudine could not have met me at a lower ebb. I welcomed the cuppa and sat on her stool with wheels, against the wall as though it was holding me up.

We chatted for ever. It was decided that I could trial her space. She was easy going and super accommodating. I used her space a couple of times, decided it wasn't for my business but we became besties from that day onward.

I convinced Claudie to come and join a new outdoor boot camp in Winston Hills, in support of my massage buddy Ian. He was leaving the physio clinic where we met and was going to give his energy to outdoor boot camps. We trained with Ian for a couple of years, until he devastatingly left us, to pursue his passion on the Northern Beaches.

Our friendship strengthened. Claudine was there to support me through all of my life's ups and downs including a divorce, my world record, my Atlantic row and all of the 2-year preparations.

She has been my daily moral support, sounding board, USA and Thailand travel buddy and rock. To check herself out of hospital, with tubes hanging out of her armpits after a double mastectomy and sit by my side during my world record is going above and beyond friendship. But that is what she did in 2018 to support me to the end of my world record million-metres row!

Claudine has had hardships like no other friend of mine. From sudden news of her 49-year-old husband having a fatal heart attack during a work function, coping with the challenges of an autistic child and the rollercoaster ride provided by her now adult daughter.

I have watched her get kicked and shoved through turmoil. What I have noticed is, Claudine is more resilient than she knows and is a survivor with fight in her that would get her through any storm.

She has a love for travel and always has something booked – something to look forward to. I do not think she will ever get to the bottom of her bucket list for travel as she just keeps adding places.

She earned the title "wifey" after Tiny passed away. Due to the demands of her very busy social calendar, I was referred to as her "plus one". Our status was upgraded to "wifey" and it has stuck.

When she met Adam, her now partner, she told him, "You have to know that I have a wife".

There are things I wish Claudine would embrace, such as the ability to say whatever she was thinking. She has a soft side that makes her tolerate more than she really wants.

The trouble with that is, it can build like steam in a kettle. Then, one day, it blows the top of that kettle with force and gusto. I have never been on the end of it personally. But Adam has. And the kids – although, they push buttons beyond acceptable with their life dramas.

She can say anything in that moment. She needs the steam, the excessive build-up to be able to let loose, and god help you if you happen to be the one to piss her off.

Like I said, it is only to specific people really, so either the saying is true – you hurt the ones you love or, they should learn to stop pushing her or she could learn to control it. All three in combo would get a great result.

I would love to see less turmoil for Claudine. I know she would thrive health-wise. It is always the status of your health that suffers when you live in toxicity or drama or turmoil.

She has done more for me than I have for her. She has stepped out of her life to come and collect me from the finish line in Antigua, sat by my side for hours every week, for 6 months while I trained for the rowing record, she made snacks and lunches and prepared the torturous ice baths for me, between rowing sets.

Claudine has been there through my expired relationships and always been on my side. Love her to death. Wish more for her – spiritually and emotionally and expect that we'll be friends for ever.

• • •

I mentioned Claudine's husband Tiny previously, a man squashed into a size 5, instead of a 6.

His large-framed figure had a personality and soul to match. He had maintained an overweight figure for many years and finally decided to undergo life-changing surgery.

He became a well-known at the local Anytime Fitness Centre and took on a whole new life style.

He was in the prime of his life with an enormous second wind of energy and zest. However, it was too little, too late. At age 49, Tiny had a massive fatal heart attack at a restaurant with his workmates.

Just like that, Claudine's life changed in an instant, and for the next 12 months she grieved that loss and tried getting on with her life, all the while running her business, and meeting and greeting people with her easy, cheerful manner.

Tiny's sudden departure left Claudine with teenage kids, Daniel and Mikaela. Her challenges got a whole lot bigger.

I remember Tiny well. He always said "don't sweat the small stuff". He loved entertaining and together, as a couple, they were super social. Tiny had some basic rules that you never dared to break, unless you wanted a dressing down. No. 1: no phones at a table where you were sharing company and a meal. He gave 100% attention to his company and expected the same. I loved that rule, because it is rare!

In his absence, Claudine maintained this social side of her life as she knew it and never said no to any invites.

I used to get exhausted just thinking of the appearances. Claudine and Tiny used to joke about what they wanted their funerals to look like. They both shared the same sentiment about not wasting money on a fancy coffin.

So, in staying true to this pledge Tiny went to rest in a coffin just that little bit on the short side. The funeral director struck up a connection with Claudine and got to know her for her ability to see the funny side and he understood her appreciation for keeping it practical.

He saved her from the hard up-sell with the fancy handles and adornments and then confessed to her that he put Tiny in a No. 5 when he really should've been in a No. 6 – so, he had to take his shoes off and put them by his side in order to fit his 6 ft 5 in frame.

• • •

OMG. Corinne and I go back to our corporate banking days at age 18.

She says she will never forget the day she met me. Dressed in a long black pleated skirt, long sleeve, white cuffed - cuff linked pin stripe blouse, hair in a bun with a 300ml of plain milk and nuts on my desk. She thought, "Fuck off, she is Miss straighty 180".

Little did we know that this moment was going to start a long-lasting friendship. Our lives have taken different paths. Hers has been raising 3 kids, being an amazing support and backbone in the business to her husband Steve. She is honest, calls a spade a spade and loves a good laugh.

I trust her opinion and know that she would never piss in my pocket – i.e. tell me what I want to hear. She just tells it how it is and often reminds that is time to get a new do or to get some new clothes. She will even take me shopping to get the new clothes.

Her wardrobe is also my wardrobe. There have been many times that she has dressed me, accessorised me and curled my hair, to help make me runway ready.

I love and cherish any time that we spend in each other's company. Give us a glass of champagne, a gin and tonic or a glass of red and look out. We can both talk under water and no matter how long we spend together, we are never lost for words.

During my preparation I would ring Rinne and use her a

sounding board, off-loading all of my latest woes. Sometimes she used to say that she would hold her breath listening to the challenges that I came up against. She felt every bit of anxiety I did. Every obstacle and hardship were endured by her. It's this support that makes you realise how lucky you are. She surely must have been sick of hearing about the boat. The boat. OMG – I often got to a point where even I was sick of the boat – and all of the woes it created. She is a breath of fresh air in my life and I need a dose of her every week.

. . .

Oli–girl is possibly the funniest chick I know. Serbian, heavy accented, ESL – a whole story on its own.

Oli is a massage buddy I met while working in a physio clinic. She has the best sayings with no intention of being funny but will have you holding your sides from laughter with expressions like "stiff like dick" – when referring to wanting to be more flexible and accommodating – she says "you know – stiff like dick man."

Her generosity to provide amazing nutrition has no limits. Oli-girl, as I call her, would seriously give you the shirt off her back. She sat by my side during the million-metre world record and would gently stuff my mouth with the measured and expected calories that I had to shovel down.

Oli is an unwavering support mentally. She listens – truly listens - and offers psychic-like feedback with real wisdom. I value her opinion and often find myself mulling over her words days later. Then they will pop up again down the track at some incident and I will think "this is what Oli was talking about!"

. . .

Where do I start with Tony – an ex, my DPA (designated person ashore, my amazing and valued friend?

How about at the very beginning?

Rewind my life to 2012 and my first solo overseas holiday, something I had promised myself since Shane and my split from a 22-year long union.

I turned 40 on Kokoda the year before and this was the year that I took myself away – by myself – for myself!

• • •

Thailand is a familiar and loved destination. I had travelled and explored Thailand extensively with Shane.

I white-water rafted, trekked, went off the beaten track, out of the tourist's comfort zone to corners I knew in which I would feel comfortable on my own.

It was to be my 41st birthday present to myself. There I was. Standing on the steps of a beach in Phuket's southernmost township, Rawai.

I was assessing the surf and the rip and the place that the Thai life savers just placed the flags – right in front of the filthiest biggest rip I had ever seen.

Just as I watched in amazement and bewilderment this tanned, fit, lean figure emerged from the shores and was strutting towards me in his pink, faded, once-red, board shorts.

"This is surely an Aussie," I said to myself. "Excuse me," I said, "Is that rip very strong, where the Thai's have just put the flags?" "Oh yeah – pay no attention, they have no idea how to read the surf," he said.

This exchange led to an hour-long conversation; me doing exactly what I said I would do. Doing things unusual to my nature.

To strike up a conversation with someone (Tony) was not

typically "me". But this was the journey I consciously chose, to do the unnatural.

After Tony discovered this was my first solo holiday and that night was my actual birthday, he insisted on picking me up from my hotel lobby to show me a sunset over the Andaman Sea that I would not forget.

My pick-up time was 6pm, from the Palms Resort. I raced through the pool area that afternoon and told the couple who I had met in our transit that we were all being picked up in the lobby, to be ready by 5 to six and that was that.

Lynn and Lionel, a 60-plus-year-old couple from the North Coast of NSW coincidentally were on my flight and staying at the same resort. I befriended them too, again part of this journey of doing the unnatural.

Tony was right. The sunset over the sea was amazing. We shared stories of our who and how we were at in this stage of our lives. We shared great Thai food and over some typically 80s classic cocktails and ended up back at Tony's for a few more drinks.

A friendship was being forged right there. What I had not planned on was the next 2 years of excitement, adventure, new experiences, new friends, new life and ultimately what became my why – to row an ocean. Tony opened the door to another world.

His life was 6 months living in Thailand and 6 months living on board his 20-year-old, immaculately maintained 42-foot fast catamaran.

He had lived this lifestyle for more than 14 years by the time I met him but he was nowhere near finished. Tony had a love and passion for travel, adventure and was fearless in skippering that vessel across the world's oceans, often single-handed. But he loved the opportunity to have company on board. He offered me this opportunity. It was a no brainer really. Of course, I could not resist although my decision-making process was not that easy.

I did agonise about stepping out of my business to live a life of – who knows what? It took me a day. That was my agonising moment and I came to a conclusion that I simply could not find a good enough reason not to say yes!

Tony and *Tactical Directions* (the boat) proved to me that we need very little in terms of material things. Living on board a boat is a minimalistic lifestyle. It agreed with me and I thrived. I learnt to sail, to fix things, learnt about preservation and conservation and most of all I learnt how much I love my freedom.

This was my newly desired life-living ambition now; to achieve the freedom to live however I like, and it was not be conventional ever again. Not 24/7 for the rest of my life anyway.

My life has to have varied and unexpected experiences or I proclaim that I am bored. Fuck that. Tony has done and seen more than any one individual I know and his bucket list is nowhere finished.

• • •

Karen and my intro was thanks to an ad I placed on flatmates. com. My advert read: "I am a working-from-home professional. My house is spotless. It is quiet. I do not have a TV. I am up at 5am every single day and am seeking a non-smoking, working professional who appreciates the same."

It was not warm and fuzzy and certainly intended to set a tone screaming, "I am not looking for a party friend or Friday night drinking buddy, not looking to make friends" and I wasn't interested in attracting someone who loves to lounge and watch TV or movies.

Perfectly, I only had one applicant. The call didn't come directly from her though. It was made by Susan, her friend, who explained that Karen wasn't in a great place at the moment so she was just helping her to remove the overwhelm of finding a place. "OH NOOOOO" my head screamed, she's a fragile basket case! That's honestly where my thoughts went. Instead, I agreed calmly and sweetly to chat with Karen and then arranged for her to view the room. Karen arrived apologising for being dressed in scrubs (she is a dental hygienist and came straight from work). She was flighty or jittery, full of a nervous energy. She liked the space, I could tell. Then she explained that she had a poodle. Hmmmmmm. Shit. A pet.

She frantically explained that the poodle was well behaved, and toilet trained; she would pick up the poo and she'd be no trouble. As a sufferer of allergies, I said I would have to meet "the pooch" Mika, a toy poodle. She was everything that Karen said.

Karen practiced a separation process. She would walk out the front door and wait five minutes, then return. She repeated this, increasing the length of time before returning. The poodle and I seemed a bit perplexed or at least I was! I thought, "Oh crap, she is surely looney toons. As it turned out, Mika is the equivalent of Karen's child. Only better than an actual child. We have formed a bond that I could not have anticipated and I love that bloody poodle now as if she is mine. I am pretty sure that the fact that I work from home, was a drawcard for Karen, so that the "oodle" (as now referred to) had company most days.

On the days that I was not to be at home, I let Karen know in advance so that she could either arrange to come home from work at lunch time (an advantage to working just three minutes from home) or she could get the grandparents to come and collect the poodle and take her back to their place for the day. I call this keeping up PR. It is great that she can rely on at least one (in fact, the only one) back up poodle minding mechanism.

Karen has rightly-so earned the title, "Best roomie in the World."

Her support during my world record was more than I could ever have asked for.

When she moved in, I still had about two months left of my

training programme. Every single Sunday I would be on that "erg" from 6am till 4pm. She would stop by and offer to get me stuff, open or close a blind, turn the fan on for me, top up my drink bladder. You name it, she supported me.

Then she turned to help the packing of provisions for my Atlantic row. That was a whole three weeks of late nights creating 90 days' worth of individual ration packs with a calculated 7,000 calories.

Every bag had to be vacuum sealed to save space. It was a time-consuming and overwhelming task, made easier with the support of Karen. Her demeanour offers a calm, stable and grounding vibe – quite opposite to my naturally higher state of excitement over everything, even a cup of tea!

Poor Karen has to hear me sigh enthusiastically out loud with every cup of tea, "Ohhhh, this is a great cup of tea" or with every mea, "OMG, that was gourmet, that was so good, you can't imagine how much I loved that."

The thing that fascinates me daily about Karen and my union is that how I ended up with a carbon copy of Shane, my ex-husband. She and he are so alike it is like living with Shane, all over again.

They both possess the same beautiful traits having not a bad bone in their body, they both never say a bad word about anyone and there is no malice in their thoughts and actions.

Annoyingly, they both share the same infuriating trait of avoidance of subjects that require "dealing with". They both would rather stick their heads in sand and hope that it went away.

I know that there is a lesson for me in this and that is why Karen has been delivered into my life by the universe. I love her and wouldn't be without her and Mika. As a result of Karen entering my world, so did JC.

Jacinta is Karen's long-distance partner. She lives in Newcastle. They do weekend visits, about 6 weeks apart. I love it when JC visits. No.10 feels complete. She is easy going, less detail-orientated and more like me than Karen. I am sure that we both must drive Karen nuts as we are less inclined to know where stuff is and think less about the detail and more about just "getting there," where or whatever that is. So many times on my boat, mid-Atlantic I would say out loud "Karen would know exactly where my iPod is." That's just how it is at home. Ever looking for something, Karen will suggest, "Look in the second drawer" and low and behold. Bingo. There it is! Second drawer!

You can totally appreciate the qualities in this amazing human. Thanks Susan, aka Poodle Susan. She is the one who reached out and answered my ad on flatmate.com on behalf of Karen. Another beautiful soul who has entered into my circle. The 6 degrees of separation display itself in this beautiful union. We three became an amazing uke-playing trio.

• • •

Think of the God Father. Dom was my first real supporter.

He is General Manager of the Boating Industry Association, father of three stunningly beautiful young adult ladies and husband to wife Shannon, a schoolteacher.

Rewind to when this "notion to row the ocean" was just in the inception stage.

Remember, May 2016 is when I decided I was going to row the Atlantic.

In June 2016 I contacted the BIA asking for some stage time to share my story, to gain some exposure in the lookout for some willing sponsors.

It took several phone calls to that office before I got to speak to Dom. After harassing his staff who had told me there simply was no stage time and that they planned these shows a full year in advance.

I just couldn't seem to take no for an answer and on the third call, Megan decided to run it by Dom.

Listening to his versions of events makes me realise what a fruitcake I sounded like. He reiterated what his great staff had already told me; that these shows are planned a year in advance.

He asked me if I would come to the show and ask for him at the door. He also asked me if I had seen any of the talks by speakers selected to go on stage to entertain the crowds. I had not, I admitted.

On arrival, after being greeted by Dom at the main entrance, he took me into their back-office space. Inquisitively, he sat opposite me and asked exactly what it was I wanted to do on stage. "Share my story" I said. "I am going to row across the Atlantic Ocean and I need some exposure to attract sponsors."

Of course, the Sydney International Boat show was a perfect opportunity with crowds of 50,000 over five days. Without laughing or smirking he said, "OK, so you have a boat?" "No, not yet" I answered. He carried on, "So, you are a rower?" "No". Hmmm – arms crossed over his chest, chin dropped, looking over the top of specs he said, "You read a book, you had a dream, you think you're going to row across an ocean, you do not have a boat and have NEVER rowed before?"

"Yep, that's right" I answered as though his was totally normal. I only then began to imagine how crazy I looked and sounded. In his final attempt to understand the magnitude of my lunacy, he said, "But you are an adventurer though?"

"No" I replied rather flatly. Feeling defeated by my own sense of how bloody ridiculous I appeared. Dom explained that the show loves people like me; we provide great entertainment. He said, "Why don't you stick around and watch Lisa Blair – she's on stage next. Lisa is the solo sailing girl planning her solo Antarctic circumnavigation.

Dom has literally been with me, supporting, giving warm and

friendly advice of how-to best deal with a sponsorship approach. He would keep my "bull at a gate" nature in check. He is and has been like a father figure in my life, without him knowing that. I value, trust and respect Dom more than words can express. From inception to conception, Dom has been a trusted source and wealth of information and contacts.

CHAPTER 7

FIRST, GET A BOAT

PREPARATION

Source a boat 2nd hand or build one - $100 000 give or take.

Complete training courses – mandatory: Survival at Sea; Sea Safety; Flares uses; Radio licence; Remote marine First Aid; Ocean rowing course; Complete 120 hours of logged rowing, in your vessel; proof of drills including competence with radio, MOB (man over board drills).

Campaign – raise $200k by attracting sponsors.

Learn to row.

Preparing to row an ocean is daunting, overwhelming and simply, a huge undertaking.

To be in the Talisker Whisky Atlantic Challenge – under the directive of Atlantic Campaigns, the governing body if you like. They set the rules and standards. You have to satisfy a whole host of rules and regulations – for your safety.

So, what does an entry fee of EURO18,500 ($A27,260) get you?

It gives you access to the group of wanna-be ocean rowers and guidance under a team of dedicated people who teach you about the practicalities, the challenges and the craziness of rowing an ocean.

It also provides the specifications to which your boat-build must adhere. By the time you reach out to them, you have pretty much already obsessed about being an ocean rower and ready to be "all in" – well, at least that's how it was for me.

The fact that you have to pay a GBP800 ($A 1,485) before they will even release any info tells them you are serious. I remember that day well. When I made the international transfer. It was like, "this is it, I am going to row the Atlantic Ocean"

...

Developing seamanship skills can only be done at sea, spending real time "on the water".

Living in Castle Hill in Sydney's North West didn't exactly give me any.

Learning to row a beautiful long, skinny, sleek rowing skull, on smooth water seemed completely opposite to any sense of reality I was in for and let's remember, I had never even rowed before.

That brings us to the introduction of the erg, a training device that causes the most professional rower or athlete to feel uncomfortable.

The indoor, stationary rowing machine can annihilate and intimidate the fittest of athletes. It is possibly the least used piece of equipment in any gym with most people saying, "ohhhh, not the rower – I hate the rower".

I used one in our training sessions at the gym and thought I was pretty good at it. The gauntlet was laid by Andrew, the ocean rower from QLD.

He suggested I attempt the World Record for the 1-million-metres row. Well, that is one way to learn the techniques.

It ticked off a whole host of other benefits: It would convert my body to the long distance, stamina endurance version that I had to become; it would certainly allow me the time to master the techniques; and more than anything, it built my mental resilience – my ability to push through pain.

It also helped me learn and refine the nutritional needs of rowing for extended periods of time, over five or six days and how to overcome the hours of mind-blowing boredom. Persistence and consistency would be the result.

The record attempt was not mandatory but it was one of the best things I did in preparation for the mental toughness it developed. It showed me I was capable of.

• • •

BOAT BUILD – the first challenge with many lessons

My decision to build the boat was made because, simply, there were none in Australia to buy.

I really did want a second-hand tried and tested hull.

The option to buy from overseas and ship to Australia, then back to the starting line and back to Australia from the finish line was a great expense.

It was cheaper to build one, apparently. My boat build was initiated by an appointed boat builder whose name I won't even disclose. It was the beginning of my stress and test of "how seriously do you really want to row this ocean?"

Andrew, my coach and mentor, willingly stepped up to be the project manager. He was going to be calling in on the build process regularly to ensure that all was going to plan.

What a mess. He rubbed the builders up the wrong way and from very early on the relationship was doomed. The workmanship was poor at best and there were inconsistencies in almost every join.

The process of building a carbon fibre boat is similar to that of fibre-glassing. You put the panels together and fill along every join with epoxy resin, a two-parr mixture that sets like concrete.

The seams and joins on my boat had glue that failed to go off, which means the ratios were wrong when they were mixing it or didn't mix it properly.

Either way, it meant that big chunks were hard on the outside and soft like marshmallow on the inside. The builders also failed to create a lovely smooth covering which meant that the tape (200gm carbon fibre cloth, soaked in epoxy resin) laid over the top had air bubbles underneath it. It was like they gave a group of pre-schoolers a tub of play dough and let them run wild stuffing it in here and there.

There were other factors contributing to the disaster. My coach, mentor and project manager – and boyfriend - was demanding changes be made to the original design, without professional consultation.

Yes, Andrew became my BF! He wore many caps.

I truly did put all my eggs in one basket. Diversifying would have been a better idea! With Andrew ordering the boat builder around and requesting certain things be changed and me being clueless, the result was an epic fail to the detriment of my boat's self-righting ability.

This only became evident though right before I had to load *Australian Maid* into the shipping container. Three weeks before to be precise.

Discovering the vessel did not self-right was a moment in time that when I really did feel defeated. I thought of giving in, surrendering to the hardships and the constant challenges placed in my way over the two years of dedication to the dream.

The feeling lasted two days. I stood up, wiped my eyes. Blood pumping, heart pounding – It was like a massive dose of adrenalin had been administered.

I was fired up; that was not how the story was going to end.

I was on the phone arranging Australia's top Naval Architect, who lived in Narrabeen, to inspect my boat and advise me why she failed to self-right.

On inspection, architect Andrew Dovell asked matter-of-factly and almost as though he knew this was the problem "Did you make any unconsulted changes to the plans during the build?

Well, Andrew did. He insisted that I buy more carbon fibre panels and have my gunwales completely enclosed, flush to the deck, so as to increase my buoyancy and storage.

Andrew Dovell said straight out, without hesitation, that this was the problem. He explained that my boat was built like a catamaran and it had to be gutted and re-tested for self-righting.

This was a massive stress. I was out of time and money. Now I had to find a boat builder who could drop tools and take me as urgent status to gut the gunwales going back to the original state, as per plans.

I had to find $10k from somewhere and then hope that this was the answer, without delay.

My team of supporters included John Smale from the Hills Men's Shed. He is one well connected fucker. He used to own boats and sold them for 30 years in Baulkham Hills. He also used to import tugboats and sell those too.

John seems to have great rapport with all the contacts in the marine world, many of whom seemed to just do favours for him. I think that says he had a good reputation.

He introduced to me the beautiful man, Joe, from Fibre Marine, in Guildford in Sydney's west. Joe said yes. He took on my boat and treated it as urgent.

On completion, he and his family even came to Pittwater to watch the roll-over test. He extended himself so generously throughout, even arriving on the day of packing my boat into the shipping container for its journey to the start line.

Joe was instrumental right up to the last minute and in every critical and crucial chapter of the boat build. To this day he continues to be a valuable and trusted go-to. In fact, I would not go anywhere else.

CHAPTER 8

OARS IN THE WATER

Launch day was in April 2017, in Manly, Queensland. It was a sensational day, a clear, blue sky-filled day.

The guys from Simrad were there to commission my electronics: chart plotter, auto pilot, VHF radio and AIS. Kenny is the guru of Simrad and went over my gear, giving it the stamp of approval.

This was also the first day that I had ever put an oar in water.

With Andrew standing in the footwell, instructing me, "drop your shoulders, lean forward, slide with your legs, relax your grip, stop winging your elbows, sit tall, slow down, calm down." The list of cues went on. He was a hard task master, but I appreciated and respected that.

I knew he was my best chance of getting a decent technique. Coming from a competitive ocean rowing background – I had actually secured the best coach. Plus, he had already rowed the Atlantic Ocean – and successfully, in 58 days.

He actually beat half of the entrants, finishing ahead of pairs and fours crew. There was mastery and confidence in his skill at the oars and as a coach.

Launch day went great. This gave us the feedback to tweak and refine the pitch of the oars, the position of my seat and was the beginning of a lot of blisters, sweat, yes – tears and a couple of good barneys. Andrew had his work cut out for himself.

The biggest error in our approach was the fact that he wore every cap: coach, mentor, boat builder, boyfriend. Talk about putting all your risk in one basket. When it a came to a sudden end I learnt the meaning of "diversify your risks".

It was a stressful relationship with the campaigning and fund-raising challenges, living in separate states and both being independent, free spirits. The additional stress of both of us being self-employed, trying to train for a world record, build a boat and tend to the normal facets of everyday life, was often overwhelming.

Andrew also had two boys. They were 15 and 13 at the time. So, he also had to try to balance a diary that included watching their football matches, having them stay over for weekends and consider their social activity as well. The logistical expense of flights to Brisbane or Gold Coast were just another splinter in your arse.

Self-employment afforded the luxury of being able to manipulate a diary, however, every day you were not on the tools, cost you $$$$.

My boat build continued beyond the World Record.

Weekends spent installing fittings and fixtures, coring out the foam and filling with epoxy resin was a tedious task but in the name of "doing a job properly", was essential to avoid squashing the foam core.

I learnt a great deal on those weekends, where I am sure I was more of a hindrance to Andrew than help, however, the experience and confidence I gained was invaluable.

Andrew was a skilled, confident, can-do anything kind of man. He seemed to just get it. Being around tools and the lingo of "fixing things" meant that I would have some basic knowledge in the event of having to fix shit at sea. Which I had to; my foot steering

Nikki and Michelle at The Boat Show

Nikki and Michelle

Nikki stretching out in the interior of Australian Maid

Nikki and Michelle on Australian Maid

Andrew and Michelle on Australian Maid

Claudine and Michelle

Claudie is a great sport who loves theme parks. Here we are in USA to celebrate her late husband, tiny's 50th Birthday.

Cat, aka, Canada

Nikki, Amy, Cat and Michelle

Michelle, Nikki and Cat

Michelle, Cat, Nikki and Amy

Michelle and Oli

Corinne and Michelle

Michelle and Corrine

Karen, Michelle and JC at The Boat Show

Michelle and JC

Michelle and Miss Molly

Julian, Osteo and friend. Long distance runner and athlete

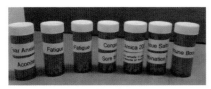

Homeopathic remedies from Molly

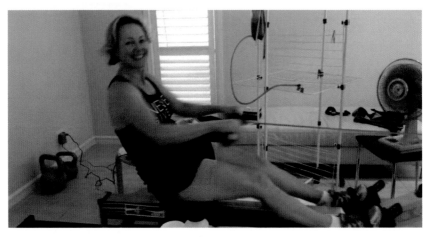

Just a regular day on the rowing machine, during my 6 month training programme. Thirteen sessions per week, included an 8 hour row on Sundays, and a 6 hour row on Mondays

Tony, my DPA (Designated Person Ashore)

Sarah and Michelle

Yes it's me, Michelle, 20 years old, at a Parramatta Leagues Club staff party

Michelle, Corinne and Jenny. We all celebrated our 21st birthdays onboard P&O's Fairstar, the Fun Ship, which was nicknamed the Fuck Ship.

My crew for Million Metre Row World Record. Support crew. These guys helped feed me, hydrate me and humour me for the duration of the 5.5 days. They were on rotating shifts 24/7. Amazing team. I could not have done it without them.

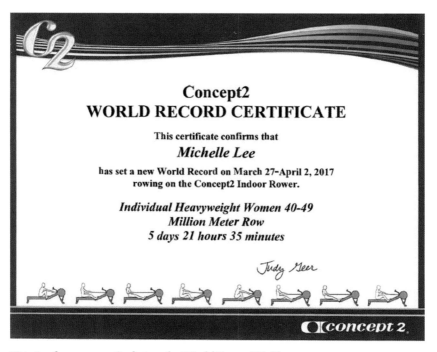

This is what you get for being the World Record Holder

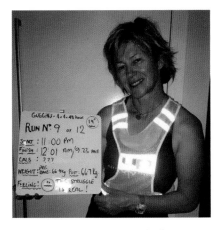 

David Goggins. 48 hour challenge:
Run 4 miles, every 4 hours, for 48
hours. This equals 5.4kms every 4
hours for 12 cycles. Run no. 9 of 12

Runs no. 10, and 12 of 12. Such sweet relief!

Training buddies, from glam to mud runs

New hiking equipment. Can't wait to try it out. Life's highlights!

Dom, who truly gave me massive support

Hiking buddies, again

Dom, Sydney Boat Show Builder

The boat building hours, and days, and weeks

Inspirational fellow adventurer, Justin Jones. Best advice gi

Jeanine Sciacca, The Silva Method instructor

Official pre race pic

D-DAY. Flying out for the start line. And the day my dad died. With my support crew.

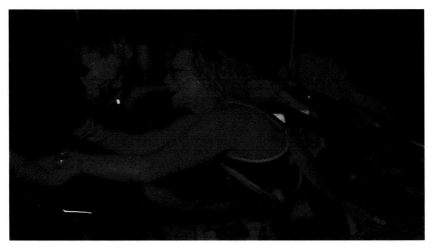

My most favourite picture in the world. My bestie Claudie, at the finish line. She was the first human contact in 68 days! Docklands, English Harbour, Antigua.

54kgs. End of race weight, and 14kgs lighter than at the start

Welcome home, thanks to the best roomie in the house, Karen

Doing what I love... speaking at schools

And here I am, reading the book that started it all. Rowing The Atlantic by Roz Savage.

Congrats from my friends and training buddies

A photo of me and Sherwood Ridge Public School Stage 3 student leaders where I spoke about the importance of persevering despite challenges, having gratitude always, and giving them a blueprint for success. A great day!

FINISHING ITEMS TO
PREPARE -

• FLAGE
• BUCKET w/ H_2O
• AUSSIE FLAG
• Q FLAG + COURTESY FLAG - already
on @ the 2nm stage.
• AUSSIE SPEEDO
• HAVE "SHORE" BAG PACKED w/
$$, SHAVER / CLOTHES items
• HAVE CABIN PACKED / SHEETS
STRIPPED / WASHING ETC.
•

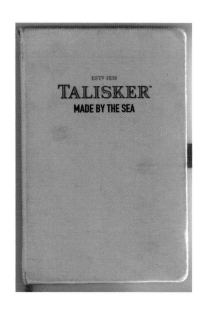

And here are a few pages from my diary
that I made sure to write on every day.

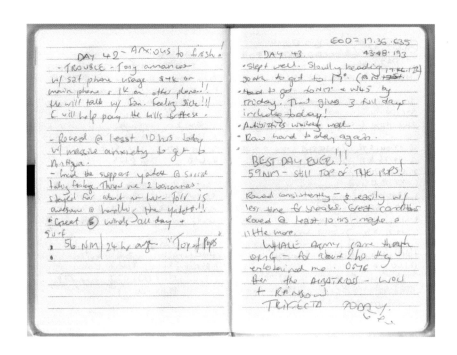

DAY 42 - ANXIOUS to finish!
- TROUBLE - Tony announces
w/ sat phone usage 84k or
main phone + 1K on other phone!!
He will talk w/ Ian. Feeling sick !!!
I will help pay the bills & these.

- Rowed @ least 10 hrs today
w/ missile anxiety to get to
Antigua.
- had the support yacht @ sunrise
today forbye. Threw me 2 bananas;
stayed for about an hour. Jolk is
awesome @ handling the yacht!!!
• Great ⊕ winds all day +
surf.
• 56 NM / 24 hr ago "Top of Pops"

EOD = 17.36 .635
DAY 43   43·48·193
• Slept well. Slowly heading (17°C·17?)
17°C·175?. Goals to get to 17°. (@ N 17.5?)
• Need to get to N17° & W45 by
midday. That gives 3 full days
include today!
• Autopilots working well
• Row hard today again.

BEST DAY EVER !!!
59NM - STILL TOP OF THE POPS!

Rowed consistently - & easily w/
less time & breaks. Great conditions.
Rowed @ least 10 hrs - maybe a
little more.
WHALE Army came through
ORIG - for about 1hr they
entertained me. 0976
Her the ALBATROSS - wow
+ RAINBOW
TRIFECTA

fell apart from the amount of torsion going through it. At least I had the knowledge of using epoxy. I knew that the two surfaces had be well scuffed for them to adhere. I knew that it had to cure – aka "go off" - and I knew that there was only a limited amount of time to work with the product before it was deemed useless.

Being at sea, away from the conveniences of "popping into Bunnings" meant that you had to adopt a mentality of not wasting anything. You had to be conscious and mindful.

This was really amplified as I neared the end of my toilet paper rations. Yes. Rations. I was rationing my rations by day 48.

Then lo- and-behold, I happened to wonder what was in the locker under my electrical box. Jackpot. It was enough toilet paper to get me to the finish line.

When shit hit the fan with COVID and through all the lockdowns – when people were buying toilet paper in ridiculous mounds of greedy fear driven behaviour, I thought, "What would they really know about rationing rations". Well, that was the point. No one would know because they acted so stupidly that some of them probably have not had to buy toilet paper to this very day.

During the boat build, Andrew made some unconsulted changes to the original plans. The tried, tested and proven plans. He called me one day with urgency, telling me to quickly make a payment to ATL composites as he had just ordered more carbon fibre panels to enclose the gunnels and produce more buoyancy and storage space.

I did not ask any questions, made the transaction and then watched my boat's design take on a whole new look. I liked the idea of more space and even more buoyancy. Little did I know that this very decision would result in a failed roll over test – a controlled capsize.

During the weeks following the failed rollover test, I questioned many things, such as Andrew saying I did not even have to do this test. He tried to deter me from performing the test. My gut, instincts and peace-of-mind all screamed that this was a non-negotiable.

There is a lot to be said about trusting your gut feeling. It rarely lets you down, I have found.

CHAPTER 9

THE START LINE

TWO WEEKS TO GO – ARRIVAL IN LA GOMERA.
I am often amazed at the coincidences and meaningful idiosyncrasies that occur and often wake me up, out of my autopilot state.

They have happened so frequently now that I find myself smiling big with a knowing that the universal energy is responding to my needs, at that moment in time.

Such as the plane trip. I finally got to the airport with Colin at the wheel, taking erroneous turns and ending up in a tizz. Gratefully, Jacinta took over with the assistance of google maps.

The ride was painful emotionally, with the news that had been delivered at 11 am that very morning, that my father passed away during emergency surgery. He had turned septic, with a twist in his bowel that had caused blood clot formations that were beyond any intervention.

I felt numb from time to time but mostly in a world of deep, aching, loss. And regret that I did not get the chance to turn up on his doorstep, boat in tow, to share the adventure I had just been on.

That was my vow; that when all this done finally, I would tow my boat up to the northern highlands where they lived alongside the Clarence River and I would take my dad out, in my great boat.

There was also guilt and a deep longing to see my brother and sister, having consciously left them to deal with the process that follows a death.

I was not going to miss my row. That was hugely selfish. There was a moment in my decision-making process where I swear, I heard my day say, "Don't you dare stand over a hole in the ground crying, go and row that ocean."

I believe I went and did it in Dad's legacy and his spirit, a man who did what he wanted, disregarded rules when they made no logical sense (within reason). He loved what he did and did what he loved. He stood for backing the underdog, standing strong in your convictions. He said what he thought and meant what he said. Basic and simple values.

He was a hard worker but loved so much what he did that I don't think he felt it was work. I remember at school being asked, "What does your daddy do?" and I replied, "He plays on machines and moves dirt around."

Officially his job title was "Earthmover", self-employed. We were taught very young that the telephone at home was for business and that we should answer it accordingly. "Hello, Ray Lee Earthmoving" and then we could rattle off the equipment my dad had and we were sure to repeat their name and number on the pad by the phone for "my dad to call you when he gets home from work". We were doing this efficiently by age seven.

Back to the plane ride. As usual, I requested an aisle seat. On the window was a youngish looking guy. I made no attempt at conversation and I guess I just looked plain sad. He reached over, put his hand on my forearm and said "if you need to talk, I am a psychologist – specializing in grief"

Again, yet another meaningful coincidence. I said flatly,

unemotionally "my dad died this morning".

He offered me the grieving process and left it at that. Wow. What are the chances really? – to be sat next to a specialist in grief.

I arrived in London, loaded up with more luggage than I have ever had on all of my holidays put together. I had boat parts and the last-minute things that I couldn't put on board before *The Maid* went into the shipping container.

I had three days in London before flying to La Gomera.

This was a great chance to catch up with an old work buddy. Having spent nearly four years in the UK from 1996, I had a decent knowledge of the layout of the land, how to get around and I had my old stomping grounds to visit. To go to some of my "favs" again. Greenwich, Streatham (where we lived) Covent Garden and of course the usual tourist haunts including Kensington Palace, St Pauls Cathedral, Houses of Westminster etc.

You now had to pay to enter most of these attractions now. Wow. Rude shock. I did not. I could not justify it, so I just looked from the outside and walked my legs off around London.

I caught up with David Ringer, a work buddy from my banking days. He was the only contact I had (through Facebook) and we had lunch – at a pub, of course. It was great to sit with familiarity and shoot shit about the old times. Man, it was 22 years ago! It always amazes me how you can catch up with an old mate and it feels like yesterday.

I remember feeling a sense of longing for the old days; the times we had living in the UK are always recalled so warmly in my memory. With my Shane, my then boyfriend. We had a great social life and didn't worry too much about anything.

With the start line always on my mind, the three days flew. Next thing I found myself waiting for the ferry, to get to La Gomera.

This moment was numbed by the recurring memory that Dad just died. The pang and wave of pain and loss would hit me and surge through my body without warning.

. . .

I was finally getting to meet Kelda. The other female solo rower.

Over the year we had gotten to know each other as we both prepared and ticked the boxes that allow you to pass go.

Again, it felt like I had known her forever. We sat on the ferry chatting about the challenge to get where we were at last. It is a milestone that you just cannot take for granted. The struggle makes you stronger, yes. That is for sure. The struggle makes you more determined than ever. You now sit back and think "I have earned the right to be here" You absolutely know that this is going to be an adventure of your life.

I was eager to just get through the next two weeks of scrutineering, meetings, pre-race last-minute scramble for compliance. I knew I had a little bit of work to do. I had sponsor stickers that still had to be placed on the hull, my race number had to go on and some minor compliance issues with a spare battery to be sourced for my VHF radio.

Meeting the rowers was a blur to me. In fact, so were a lot of the pre-race meetings. My mind was heavy with thoughts of my brother and sister, back at home arranging the farewell for Dad. Knowing that they were in their own world of pain increased my suffering. Having painful phone calls with them and the guilt of my selfishness weighed heavily and came over me in unexpected waves.

Kelda and I shared accommodation on board a sailing boat in the local marina.

It was perfect in every way. The location put us super close to the meeting tent and got us in the zone for small, confined spaces. We self-catered and socialized minimally. Kelda already knew a good handful of the other rowers as so many of them were from the UK. They had been on courses with each other and the start line was like a mini reunion.

For me, it was a reminder of my first week in high school, when I didn't know anyone and had to find my groove.

For the first time I really felt alone as I watched the teams and crew complete tasks so efficiently with the luxury of sharing them amongst themselves.

I have never been totally comfortable in large social settings and struggled with interacting and connecting with the bulk of the rowers.

There were 84 of us, from 14 countries. I became closest to my neighbouring buddies on the "hard stand". Our boats were all lined up on cradles in order of number of crew on board. On my right I had *Au Large*, a pairs boat with two beautiful young French gents and then the mad trio on my left – two amazingly fun and outgoing British chicks and a very vibrant Canadian. We helped each other and borrowed tools and ideas with final, last-minute preparation, organisation and chart plotting.

CHAPTER 10

READY, SET

SCRUTINEERING

The purpose of scrutineering is to ensure that all crew have EVERY item on board as set out inr the Ocean Rowing Manual.

It is a two-hour procedure where every item is laid out on a tarp and then meticulously ticked back by one of the duty officers.

The items to be checked off are all rations, spares kits, grab bag, medical kit, batteries, sat phone, tool kit, life jackets, life line, PLB's, EPIRBS, flares, cooking / gas cylinders, clothing, paper charts and of course your bucket – aka, toilet.

A duty officer goes over the hull, inspecting grab lines, hatches, electrical items, storm anchors. Every line is measured; 70 metres towing line; 90 metres parra anchor line; 125 metres retrieval line; anchor plus 6 metre chain and 10 metres of line.

It was a huge job; the off-loading of the items and then of course, putting them all back on board.

As well, I had to load the bottom of my hatches with 150 litres of ballast that would also act as my emergency drinking water in the event of my electric water-maker failing. Making space for the 300 individual 500ml bottles was just another challenge.

Somehow, it all fitted back on board and in fact gave me another opportunity to shuffle my weight and better distribute it.

With a huge sigh of relief, I passed my inspection with just one item to source, a spare battery for my VHF hand held radio.

Tim, another solo off a boat called *Tame the Kraken* arranged it for me, as he too needed the same battery.

There was a sense of comradery at the start line and a genuine feeling that we all truly just wanted each other to cross the finish line. My competitor was the solo Kiwi rower, Isaac. He was in an older version of my boat. Same design except his was built in plywood and mine the lighter carbon fibre.

Being the only other Woodvale design meant that we were equal in terms of boat performance. His boat was a right mess. It needed a lot of work, a piece of rotting wood in the hull had to be repaired and it just looked plain grotty. I think I was surprised that he actually passed in time, to row out on 14 December.

He had no clue that I was obsessed with beating him. I used him as my motivation to stay true to giving it 100 per cent effort and he kind of kept me honest with my hours on the oars. With every satellite phone call back to Tony, I would ask "where is the Blue Rower?" I wanted the stats on how far behind me he was. I guess you could say I do have a competitive side to me and I do like a challenge.

• • •

With all my kit laid out, I stood back and was consumed with a huge emotion of overwhelming gratitude to the people who had helped make this happen.

I felt like a spoilt brat and almost undeserving. My food rations, packed with the help of my friends, over hours, over weeks. My roomie, Karen, was there at every milestone, supporting both morally and physically.

The energy and time that they gave was staring me in the face. Claudine from Million Metre training to everything stressful, celebratory, through all of the highs and lows; so many did so much.

Getting to the finish line would be the smallest token of appreciation the I could give back. No pressure.

Next step of the start line excitement is to be put in the water.

My turn came. Together, other rowers helped wheel my boat to the ramp and launch me, on board, into the water. I proudly rowed her to my designated slip on the marina and installed my rudder with pins. This was now also an opportunity to go for a row, to run the water-maker and ensure that the autopilot was calibrated.

I had spent months on board my boat in the lead up to reaching the start line. Every weekend constantly for five months I would spend two or three nights, rowing around Pittwater and The Spit.

I would practice man -overboard drills, cleaning my hull, using my radio and generally just getting used to being on a confined space. I would stay in a beautiful bay on anchor or pick up a public mooring to enjoy the rocking and water against my hull. This was always a joy and I reminisce warmly about the peace and serenity of being surrounded by beauty of Sydney's foreshores.

The rule book stipulated that each rower must spend a logged 96-night hours on board. My logged hours went way over and beyond. It became my weekender. I felt confident inside the safety of the harbour but I knew that I would not be able to experience losing sight of shore. I knew that I would have to leave that one in the "world of firsts" chapter.

My time spent on board required me to practice weather routing, ensuring that I studied the winds, tides and forecast. One of the obstacles I had to deal with constantly was taking into account what way the wind blew and the strength. My boat is not a coastal rowing vessel. Being seven metres long means that I have a huge windage and can easily be blown into a land mass.

To avoid having to be rescued, I had to carefully choose my rowing route based on my ability to row against either wind, tide or both.

**The last thing I wanted
was to be rescued**

CHAPTER 11

ROW

**14 DECEMBER 2018. WEATHER: FAVOURABLE
CONDITIONS. DEPARTURE: 3.05PM.**

The final meeting was at 7 am. All rowers gathered for the last time for a weather update and reminder of the departure procedure.

We were given the seven-day forecast and received a touching speech from race organiser, Carston, and our race duty officers.

This was it. We were set to go with a great outlook.

As we made our way down the marina, families walked arm in arm with their brave adventurers. I walked alone, in a state of strange calm. I watched the families and partners cling on to each other in a desperate embrace to hold this memory to last until they met again at the finish line.

I imagined what it would be like to have someone by my side and decided that I liked my solo position.

I don't think I could've handled the overwhelming feelings associated with that last kiss, hug or touch. It would've been too painful. I had hours to go before it was my turn. It felt a bit surreal. The docks were a buzzing with an energy of dread, for the loved ones left behind to wait until their rower returned home safely, of excitement, relief that the day had finally arrived and of course anxious nerves.

This was the first time that most of us had experienced losing sight of shore on board our tiny row boats.

We had all spent about two years getting to the start line. We had all sacrificed social events, watched our spending (or spent everything we earned on the boat) and generally obsessed about this moment for at least two years.

As I watched the first crew of five row past me, out of the marina and into the harbour of La Gomera I just felt numb. I felt like time stopped. I couldn't believe that in a few hours, it would be my time.

I snapped myself out of my stupor and cheered and clapped as the next 5's came through. This was to take a couple of hours. I chatted with a couple of the other crews, bid them a great crossing and tried to savour the moment and hype and energy.

Finally – the solos' turn.

The youngest of the teams went first - Lucas, a young handsome lad from the UK. He had a quiet confidence about himself, and I knew he would do well. Then Tim, from *Tame the Kraken* – an English dude, living in the USA and about my age. He had a wife and two kids who flew to the start line to see him off. He had a brand-new Rannoch boat. He was cool and calm and seemed to have it all under control. Tim also had a mate fly in to help him at the start line.

The moral support of a buddy at the start line would've been a sweet luxury.

Timmy went past me and I decided it was time to take to my deck. Kelda was number three of us five solos. She seemed ready. After having radio issues and requiring a brand new one she managed to take it in her stride. She was rowing as a disabled rower. One of her ankles was fused and had no flexion or extension. She had her foot plat adapted to accommodate her inflexibility and immobility. She rowed a donated boat, tried and tested with a couple of crossings under her hull. What a gift. She fancied herself as bit of a solo operator.

She had been on the UK paralympic team for kayaking and had a tough determination about her character. In the end, Kelda took an amazing additional 10 days. She was the hero and super star. Everyone had so much admiration for her and every extra day she was out there beyond my finish date, my heart ached a little for her.

She struggled with the isolation from day 2, which really surprised her. I remember the realisation hit me on day 23, when I thought, "I'm a bit over me".

I had a little chuckle at myself as I asked, "is this all you have, Shell?".

• • •

Rower number four of five. Me.

Oh crap, I still had my fenders blown up and attached to my boat. In a wild frenzy, the race officials each squished the air from my fenders and threw them on my deck.

A final chat, well wishes and boom, they pushed me off the safety of the marina.

With a huge crowd cheering and waving a bag of oranges was flung onto my deck from someone in the crowd. Wow. What a magnificent gesture.

I couldn't believe my luck. I was laughing and thinking, "I can't believe it, I'm going, this is it!" It all felt unreal.

The Blue rower, Isaac from NZ, was last away. The funny thing that struck me was the direction that everyone seemed to take.

I looked at Kelda and Isaac and thought, "Oh my god, what are they doing?"

I wondered if they knew something that I did not. My route

was carefully planned with Tony. I did not know anyone else's strategy. When I heard myself verbalise that out loud, I instantly felt relieved. I had my own race to run and course to follow.

I had to trust in my own plan and carry on in a southerly direction. I rowed calmly and thought about the last two weeks; the crews that I had the pleasure of meeting, my time spent with Kelda as a roomie, the two Frenchie's who were parked next to me on the hard stand, being able to meet the team from Atlantic Campaigns who had held our hand during the preparation process.

I regretted not spending any time sightseeing La Gomera. I thought how cool it would be to return to La Gomera one year to see the rowers off. To be able to offer my assistance to the solo rowers. Be their gofer.

I rowed into the night and ate my snacks so that I didn't have to stop to prepare a meal.

The plan was to row as long as possible to get 40 nautical miles south before hanging a right and changing my direction to head south west.

The weather was perfect for my auto pilot and angle that I wanted. Life was good.

I think it was about 1am when I decided to turn in. I wiped myself with a fresh=water soaked and wrung cloth and settled in for my first night of 68.

· · ·

A crack of thunder crack and a wild tossing of my little 7.7m boat woke me from my slumber.

That is Mother Nature for you. She can change and startle you. She goes with you and against you. The best thing you can do, is work out how to best utilise the conditions to maintain your objective. In my case, that was hold as much west in my bearing as possible.

Knowing how your vessel handles in terms of wind and where the wind hits your panels can help you with selecting a bearing to hold that maximises your forward motion.

I had done a little bit of sailing so knew by feel how to achieve this. Even though it was frustratingly inaccurate at times, I learnt that the wind always clocks around in your favour. This was a constant lesson in acceptance of the things you cannot change.

Eventually I decided to put a call in to the race duty manager. There were two of them, Ian and Lee.

They were part of the crew that made up Atlantic Campaigns. They were on a roster that ensured the sat-phone was manned 24/7.

Lee answered my call. He said, "hello, hello. It's the Australian. You are the second last of the fleet to call in."

Apparently, they receive calls early on as the crews develop their routine and get used to their new life on the ocean. He called it a comfort call. I loved the fact that I was the second last. All other crew had called in earlier and the Kiwi and myself had been humming along.

I asked him how everyone else was doing and said that it was raining, rough and we had thunder. I am sure he was laughing at how green we were. Not laughing in the sense that he was making fun of us, but more of a knowing that our nerves were on edge and he knew that it would only require another 24 – 48 hours and our new routine would be established.

The adaptation period happened in 48 hours for me. I stuck to the same routine that I developed in that first 48-hour period. I was shocked at how quickly it was developed. The adjustment period differed between the crews and individuals. I attributed mine happening so fast to having spent so many hours on board my boat in the months leading to the start line.

The fact that I had missed out in 2017 and had to wait another year was a blessing in disguise.

CHAPTER 12

SUNRISES, SUNSETS, RAINBOWS AND STARS

LIFE ON THE OCEAN WAVES

The days were assured of brand-new dawns, sunsets that made you ooohhh and ahh, night skies with countless falling stars, a Milky Way that lit the water up like a highway and uninterrupted rainbows as I'd never seen before.

To say I was in awe is an understatement.

To have a full moon on a clear night with the ocean as flat as a tack was a spectacle that I promised myself to lock into my mind's eye, for recall at a time when you need inspiration or gratitude.

My 68 days indulged me with three full moons. Each one was perched in a crystal-clear sky. It completely outshone the stars. It lit up the ocean and elevated my emotion to pure joy, wonderment and gratitude.

The galaxy of stars never disappointed either. There were many nights I would lay in my cabin, under the hatch and watch a falling star that looked as though it was falling on my boat.

The sunsets were a spectacular live show, with me in the front row every time. The going down of the sun was welcomed by the thought that I was one day closer to the finish line. It was also my favourite part of the day as I rowed naked, air-drying from my 750ml fresh water bath from a black plastic drinking bottle.

Each morning I would fill the bottle with fresh water and leave it on deck in the sun. By 6.30pm it was hot. I would strip off and suds myself up to remove all of the layers of sunscreen accumulated from the day, then rinse myself with the 750 mls. This was a luxury that most crew did not enjoy.

You see, water is precious. It costs energy from your power source. As making drinking water is the priority, rinsing your body by each crew member would be impossible to maintain.

I used to make about 12 – 15 litres per day, which meant running my water-maker for three hours cost 12 amps. It was part of my maintenance schedule, knowing your energy expenditure and daily needs.

If there was inadequate sun due to extended periods of cloud cover, you would have to be conservative with your power usage. That might mean turning off your auto pilot and manually foot steering and turning off navigational equipment like the chart plotter and row with your eye on the magnetic compass.

All of this became second nature. Checking your battery management system for the voltage of your batteries and knowing how many amps each individual item costs is essential knowledge. I was lucky. My boat was wired so well that I had zero problems electrically and never had to sacrifice systems for power conservation.

Having a basic knowledge of how to wire the boat is a massive advantage. I had watched every wire being hand-clamped and heat-shrunk. It gave me massive peace of mind. Watching it was also like doing it.

There is proof of the power of visualising a technique and the effect it has on the brain. Dr Joe Dispenza has conducted many studies of people learning how to play a keyboard. Two groups are used – one is told to watch tutorials while the other group has actual lessons on the keyboard. At the end of the study, they conclude that the visual group's brain has changed in the same manner as if having played the keyboard.

This is great news for me and I took comfort in knowing that the brain was taking in so much just by watching. So, with this knowledge I learnt a lot by studying videos. It is a powerful piece of information and can be applied practically in all aspects of your life. Dr Joe also proved that you can achieve muscle growth by using your imagination of performing bicep curls. They have measured the physical growth and strength. How freaking amazing is that!

Sea life frequented my space daily. Between the fish life under my boat and the bird life, I was never alone.

Frequent bird life had a significant and profound effect on my mood. It would intrigue me and leave me wondering where they were going, how they rested, fed and slept between 5,000 kms of this body of water.

Long after their departure I would be pondering their existence. I had a strong sense that it was my dad, coming to visit and chat with me. Initially it was distressful. I found myself overwhelmed with emotion as I felt it was my dad.

His death on the morning of my departure was sudden to say the least. He was supposed to die then, that day. I imagined that the bird was Ray, watching over me. Great comfort would blanket me by day seven. He was looking over me and protecting me from any nasty weather. He kicked my pants when I needed it and consoled me when I felt despair.

My daily encounters with the birds were a highlight and joy. I would call out and whoop and sing to them. My encounters were captured on video for my reminder when I need an uplifting moment in my normal Monday to Friday world.

The going down of the sun also reminded me that tomorrow was another chance to get it right. All of my failings and shortfalls from one could be refined and tweaked the next. I still say that now, back in the normal hum drum of 9-5. It gives me inspiration for the new day.

• • •

Rainbows always filled me with an awe and made me think about the water particles passing through the sun's rays.

Knowing they are an optical illusion and they depend on where you are situated in relation to the source of light creates a sense of contradiction in my mind.

I tried to remember my science teacher, Mrs Marshall, standing in front of me explaining the refraction and reflection principles that determined the bend. Known as the arc of the rainbow and the refractive index effect on the radius. Man – I just could not recall the facts.

I would sing the song, "I can sing a rainbow – red and yellow and pink and green. Purple and orange and blue." I would always think of the pot of gold at the end of the rainbow, an Irish legend that sparked the imagination of my child mind.

Every rainbow viewing heard me say out loud, "I knew this was not going to be all rainbows and butterflies." With most rainbows, wind and rain were associated. Squalls would come at me or around me most days, sometimes multiple times. If they were in my direction of travel, I would welcome them for the additional wind they gave me, assisting me heading westward.

If they were beam-on (hitting me on the port or starboard side), I would curse and carry on for that meant that I was being pushed North or South.

Squalls also meant rain which meant a wash for my solar panels and deck. I always welcomed the opportunity to wash the salt off my solar panels. The crusty formation and build-up of salt would affect the charging capability of the panels.

My housework included a daily soft-cloth wiping to ensure efficiency of my panels. Compared to the demands of living in suburban, first world living, my housework was over in a jiffy; a quick rinse of my deck, a damp cloth-wipe over of my cabin and the occasional bucket style hand wash of my limited clothing items.

I had no dust to wipe or the grime and filth from pollution. All in all, I spent more time on maintenance, checking for loose nuts and bolts or from chafe on my steering lines, making water and meal prep.

Obviously refuelling was priority and thanks to my preparation, my caloric needs were all taken into consideration. Ensuring 7,000 calories meant that I had to maximise my calories through high carb, high protein dense combinations.

The million-metre row training helped enormously with this prep, learning the importance that nutrition had on performance.

CHAPTER 13

GOOD AND BAD DAYS

MAKING GOOD – IN BAD

Days are rated good or bad, based on the number of miles rowed.

On a good day, I covered 50 NM and on a bad day I only covered 17 NM. Bad days were those when mother nature was not delivering favourable conditions and a conscious decision had to be Made, "to make bad good".

The difference is wind, either the direction, the strength and the waves.

Direction plays a massive role in the performance of your boat. In a perfect world you would have a following sea with winds blowing in the same direction and they were pushing you on the bearing that you wanted, of course, pointing straight to the finish line, as the crow flies.

Ha-ha, dream on, my friend! If you listened to the experts who talk about trade winds and currents you soon learn that what is text-book "typical" is rarely what you get.

You see, we should have had predominately easterlies and flowing seas. What really happened was wind against wave, waves hitting you beam-on, meaning the side of the hull is getting smashed with different volumes of water under varying pressure.

This makes rowing A challenge as you often have one oar in and one out. It puts you on a skewed angle so that your hip, lower back or shoulder is prone to some kind of injury through the imbalance of your weight on the rowing seat.

It is extremely bumpy and less than pleasant. The wind and waves take a while to catch up to each other after they have lost sync.

The one thing I did learn, was that they will ALWYS clock around, to be working in perfect harmony with each other – EVENTUALLY.

. . .

Here comes the lesson of patience and acceptance over resistance. After fighting this conflict of direction for two days, I finally rang my DPA, Tony, and said "this is impossible to maintain," My lower back was copping a hammering due to the camber I was rowing on as the waves hit me on the port side trying to push me North, while the wind was hitting me from the starboard.

Eventually I had to go with the flow and take the path of least resistance. It means you may lose miles and have to make up for it on the change.

There are also storm strategies that you can adopt which include deploying a drogue from the stern or a parachute anchor from the bow. The drogue would be used in the event of huge following seas and winds, especially if you feared pitch poling – that is being tossed down the face of a wave stern over bow, i.e. arse over tit. The other storm strategy, the parra anchor is deployed from the bow if you were in headwinds and losing ground, being blown backwards. Very demoralising to say the least.

I am pleased that I did not lose miles, not once!

These anchors are essentially a series of canvas cones – or one big cone – attached to about 90 m of line. The setup is from a bridle system off stern or bow. It is a really great piece of kit that saves lives.

You hope never to use it. It is one of those things that you would rather have and not need, than need and not have.

I used the drogue a couple of times for steering and stabilising my direction.

The seas were so minimal in movement that the auto pilot could not work efficiently. The auto pilot was named "Angel". She makes life much easier on any boat, however, all the gear on a rowing boat has to be adapted as it is all made for vessels that travel 7, 10 and 12 knots and above! That means that they labour on our little 1-3 knot travelling, human powered vessels.

My auto pilot was used very conservatively to day 34. Then, after a stern talking to by Tony, I never turned her off! I ran her 24/7 from day 34. She lasted the whole distance. I treated her like gold and made adjustments to the angle of my boat in relation to the sea conditions. In order for her not to burn out I would change my bearing to accommodate the efficiency of her motor.

I attribute this to the fact that she lasted. Every time I could hear the motor working frantically or abnormally, I would crack off a degree or add some. Wait. Listen. And carry on. There is a philosophy that says, "If you treat your equipment well, it will treat you well."

It goes for friendships, relationships and was true and evident in the mere fact that she got me home and I still use it today!

CHAPTER 14

WORST DAY EVER

DRAMA QUEEN MOMENT – DAY 46

Many of us are inclined to have a DQ moment at some point.

This is when you overreact, become irrational and lose sense of reason and logic.

My diary on day 46 says: "Worse day EVER!!!!!!" It was a day when everything just seemed to compile. I had an earache, a tooth ache, the biggest seas coming at me from the beam while the wind was behind me.

My nerves were irritated with the constant blowing wind. I had half a dozen squalls before lunch and to top it off, the seas and skies were dark grey. It felt overwhelmingly bleak and miserable.

My anxiety was sky high, confidence knocked and the possibility of finishing this race seemed threatened by the fragility of my frazzled mind.

I don't mind a challenge. I accept that some days are better than others.

I knew this situation wasn't life threatening and yet I couldn't self-regulate to a calm state of mind. Poor Tony had the sat-phone calls with me a blubbering mess. He patiently listened, offered solutions and tried to bring focus to the good things – that my auto pilot was working, that my water-maker was working, that I was not in threat of capsizing.

No matter what he said, I just wanted my DQ moment.

The strange thing with these moments is that you can see the funny side, when homeostasis has been restored.

The situation was a combination of being tired, exhausted and just wanting a cuddle. I missed human touch. I wanted to hold someone's hand. My need for human connection was now all I could think about.

Yes. My tooth and ear were aching but it was 10 times worse, in my perception. Change your attitude and your perception changes.

A good night's sleep and bowl of hot custard with an earl grey tea proved to be the trifecta I needed.

The next day afforded me the luxury to reflect on Day 46 with some humour. I decided that I definitely had a case of the Drama Queens. With some very conscious effort, joy, ease and grace were restored. I reminded myself not to let my anxiety take control and to enjoy the moments – until next time.

• • •

Tantrums, tears and drama queen moments continued throughout the duration.

It is amazing what sleep deprivation does to you and how it effects your capacity for reason and logic. I remember a time when I was bawling my eyes out, in the middle of eating my tuna from the tin with a rice cake in the other hand.

I was filming with the Go-Pro. I have no idea what I was crying about as the wind was interfering with the mic. I laughed like crazy at myself, together with my roomie, when I was watching my hundreds of videoed moments.

The joke was that you can never let a good old-fashioned cry get in the way of eating! It then reminded me of when I was consoling my heart broken GF from her recent (that day) break up. I said, "Let me take you to dinner, I'll pick you up and we will go and have a nice Thai". As if she felt like eating. She couldn't eat or think straight. She felt like her world had come to a standstill when the drop-kick (nick-named Pony tail boy) dumped her through text message.

Let me set the scene. When Claudie described his appearance, I couldn't help but laugh, hysterically, and for way too long. Inappropriately in fact. He had a ponytail with about five elastics in it separating or controlling it to the end. It was short at the front and sides. He was short and really skinny. He had something wrong with his shoulder and was kind of all hunched forward. When he ate he slumped over his plate. Oh, and he had funny teeth or something. Hmmm. Say no more. Hey. I knew Claudie would outgrow him, she just couldn't see it. Of course, as with hindsight, she can see it now and laughs madly at the description of the hunchbacked ponytail guy.

Anyway, back to the dinner; while she sat there all sad and forlorn, I ploughed my way through the dishes ordered for two and then took her home. The point being? Food and I are a big part in each other's lives. I obsess over it actually. Can be eating breakfast and talking about what is for dinner while remembering how good a meal was fives ago.

I want to explain the power in words. The diary entry of day 46 – "Worse day EVER!!!" – disturbed me for days and kept me thinking and anchored to it.

I had to ask myself what was it about that bloody entry. After the day had been and gone. I got through it. I was in a much better mindset.

So, why did it create such a negative vibration in my body? I figured it out and had to remedy it. By crossing out the word EVER, I instantly felt better. It really proved to me the strength and vibration words have, positively or negatively. Massive lesson learnt.

Remember, the words you speak and the tone you add will bring more of the same back to you. It is a ripple effect or better than that it is like a Ricker Shae.

CHAPTER 15

THE CHOCOLATE STASH

LOCKER NUMBER 6: REWARD, MORALE BOOSTER AND FEEL-GOOD FACTOR ENHANCER

My meals were a highlight and gave me something to think about while doing yet another three-hour rowing shift.

I would go through my meal options: green chicken curry, spaghetti bolognaise, vegetable pasta, Moroccan pork and couscous, beef and black bean, lamb casserole, chicken tikka, tuna salsa and rice.

Rice was added to most meals as it was a good calorie addition.

There were some universal lessons I learnt living on board a boat/ yacht? during my 2013 and 14. If you asked any sailor what are the two things that you obsess over? They would reply: 1. The weather; 2. What meal to prepare next.

This can create an all mind-consuming distraction. The available items in the dry stores, fridge or freezer affects the outcome and experience.

There are times when you are down to your last onion, tin of chick peas, bag of frozen veg and a frozen portion of spaghetti bolognaise that you impressed those on a neighbouring anchored vessel with. Entertaining on a yacht often means that someone will supply the salad, another person the main and you might both chip in to create some kind of portion-controlled dessert. Pretty much, you always take your own drink in a Sippy cup.

It is little different on an ocean rowing boat.

The obsession with food is probably even greater, as it gives the mind something else to occupy it's pain filled, human-touch craved state.

When I trekked the Kokoda Trail, meal times were absolute highlights, welcomed by the beings that resembled inexperienced city slickers but who were now rough, rugged, often limping, bedraggled, filthy, weary but bloody happy civilians travelling in the footsteps of our grandfathers' fight for freedom.

I remember so well how amazing two-minute noodles were as they slid around on my dinner plate. Yes, dinner plate, because at the time I didn't have the energy to find my bowl or cup – pouring the satchel of chicken flavouring on top and slurping them up like a deranged animal that hadn't eaten in months.

My point is, adventuring makes every single meal seem gourmet, especially if it is hot. In essence,

adventuring makes you feel more gratitude for the things that we can so easily take for granted.

...

I lived for meal times on my boat.

Footnote: Kokoda Track is the current official gazetted place name used by the Papua New Guinea Government and the Australian War Memorial. Before and during the Second World War the route was variously called track, trail and road, and so there seemed no standardised name at the time.

They were more than something that you shovelled in your mouth. Meals were a reward system.

Locker number 6! This was where the stash of whole jars of Nutella and peanut butter were. There were also kg slabs of fruitcake on board and umpteen packets of dried figs, mangos, trail mix and biscuits.

I would "allow" myself access to the treasure only if I had done a great rowing shift, without stuffing around, without getting out of my rowing position to see the fish under the boat or checking my chart plotter or insisting on wiping my solar panels over.

There are many things that you can to do distract yourself and take your focus from what you are doing.

This showed in my results – my miles rowed, or not!

So, I invented the reward system and used the white board, for accountability.

By rowing to my recorded and timed miles on the white board, I was able to show some good and consistent numbers.

One of the biggest issues I created was breaking into my snack packs before the designated day.

At 2 am I would sometimes find myself searching for a bar, usually marzipan chocolates that were scattered through my packs, in no sequenced order.

I did run out of my individual packs by day 52. For this I was grateful for locker No.6 even more. At least now I know what I craved the most.

Obviously, I will be rectifying this dilemma next time round.

There I go again, saying "next time." I actually used to say "when I row another ocean" as though it was gospel that I would be doing another!

Then, the funny thing was when I finally made land for at 9.30 pm on day 68, I said to my bestie minutes after stepping off my boat "Don't ever let me something like this again – without you!"

The seed was planted and the idea was to plague me, yet again. Another great thing about expeditioning or adventuring is that it gives you a licence to eat whatever you like, and still lose weight. Your appetite is a never-ending mind consuming beast.

CHAPTER 16

FIRST WORLD PROBLEMS

SOCIAL MEDIA, RADIO, NEWSPAPERS, MOBILES, EMAILS – THE COMPONENTS UNDERLYING MANY FIRST WORLD PROBLEMS.

When you remove all of life's distractions, such as social media and your phone, you're just left with the raw 'you' and you get to explore the things that really matter, like your friendships. It's a good way to reassess and re-evaluate what's important to you."

Now this is heaven, right? Do it for a day and I absolutely guarantee you will feel different.

Some may need more than one day to even begin to appreciate it and I believe the more shit and crap you have going on in your life, the more difficult this will actually be!

The more devices that hold you like a vice will mean a tougher time in transition from overload to peace and calm.

I have come to realise that people generally struggle with silence and minimal interruptions. I knew I would love it.

I have not owned a TV since 2011. I do not read a newspaper and I do not listen to the radio. My lack of curiosity is both genuine and sincere. I do not care what is happening in mainstream media BS.

Imagine a world where no one can hound you, demand anything from you. No phone calls requiring your attention. Imagine being completely in your own head, uninterrupted and free from the demands of absolutely ANYONE! Imagine existing without obligation to be anywhere or speaking to anyone. Or, how about, having ZERO exposure to pollution, dust, household bleaches, cleaning aids, chlorine.

Man. I was seriously living this pollution-free life with maximum doses of Vitamin D and not to mention the therapeutic value of being on the water.

I want to touch on this for a moment.

Consider we have 70-80% of our body made up of water. Water is affected by the moon in its phases.

With those two thoughts in mind, consider that psyche wards workers can tell hair-raising stories about the moods and changes they see on the wards during a full moon. Water responds to vibration.

The book *"The hidden messages in water"* by Masuru Emoto examines the theory of the effects words, tone and vibrational energy have on water.

Taking water particles, freezing them and then studying them under a microscope can show the distinct formations caused by the vibrations created by such things.

It is a fascinating and proven phenomenon that you simply cannot deny. Water holds properties that have cured anxiety, lowered blood pressure and create calm to a fractured mind. Remember; It covers more than 70% of the Earth's surface, makes up nearly 70% of our bodies, and constitutes over 70% of our heart and brains – not surprising then that the mere sight and sound of water can induce a flood of neurochemicals that promote wellness, increase blood flow to the brain and heart and induce relaxation.

Knowing those amazing properties of water, imagine seeing

nothing but water. No land in sight. Just the shades of blue ranging from turquoise to deep dark crystal blue of an ocean, thousands of metres deep.

Welcome to my water world. As a severe sufferer of dermatitis and eczema my skin has ensured that I have endured almost a lifetime of pain and discomfort. Being in the middle of the ocean, free from the natural oil-stripping frequent and all too regular chlorine rich showers, proved to be the perfect and most physically satisfying game changer.

My skin has NEVER glowed such utter health and well-being before and pain-free!

We loved this sun drenched, wellbeing-boosted environment more than I could ever have imagined. It agreed with me and for the first time in my life I looked awesome; more specifically, my red, sore, itchy, dry skin did!

Another realisation was crystal clear – the external stressors in our environment cause disease and dysfunction. Ocean rowing is a never-ending dose of nature-rich, pure goodness.

Just looking at bodies of water in nature have been proven to lower cortisol levels – the stress hormone in our bodies.

Boaters will testify to this. They know that their mood changes instantly when they are back on the water. The addiction is real.

Now, can you imagine adding another element to this – meditation.

I will be meditating daily, surrounded by the ocean, in different conditions. My boat is frequently visited by inquisitive dolphin pods, whales, numerous fish species and bird life.

Add uninterrupted rainbows, cloud formations that can have you ooohhing and arrhh-ing over and then solitude, sometimes deafening.

CHAPTER 17

DOUBTS AND DOUBTERS

There were times when the sense of overwhelm was so great that my chest was tight. I could feel myself almost panting and had to remind myself to breath. Just breathe.

FILTERS AND WHITE BOARDS, AND "PUT A FRESH HEAD ON"

Having a filter to help control your mind is essential to successfully navigate your way through life. Being able to diss the negativity and the nay-sayers is a skill, once learned, that removes limits and boundaries.

Being able to "not give a fuck" about what others think of you, is the most freeing attributes anyone could hope to master. At least – that is what I have come to conclude.

The number of times I was called crazy during my preparation was a true test of how much I really wanted to row an ocean.

There were bets I would not make it. Many a sailor told me that my boat would make it – but my mind would let me down.

As my departure date loomed closer than I could keep up with, I was struggling with the pressure of the comments and my own little birdie on my shoulder started to chirp.

The old imposter syndrome rose up and filled my head with doubts.

This is when I realised that the power of the mind control was required.

By creating a filter and being more conscious of to whom and what I listened, I found that the anxiety levels dissipated to a level that enabled me to think clearer.

It is impossible to recall things when you are in distress. It wasn't serving me and I knew that I had to get a grip on the situation.

It was this moment that thought of speaking to Justine Jones, "Jonesy", an adventurer.

I had watched and admired his adventures – paddling across the ditch from Australia to NZ and some crazy arse skiing across the ice coast of Antarctica to the South Pole and then a nice little walk across Australia with wife Lauren and baby – yes, a baby – pushing a cart from the bottom of Australia to the North.

This is someone who knew of the preparation, fundraising, mental anguish, solitude and sacrifice and of the what-to and what-not-to do's. I knew I had to start to create a filter of who I let in and what information was going to serve me in my quest for the last push to the start line.

I had seen Jonesy a few times around the traps, at boat shows and had reached out to him via email or a call. I even turned up at a conference in Newcastle simply because he was the guest speaker on stage. I had no idea what the conference was. As it turned out, it was a trade night for the travel industry. I stood out like dogs' balls as everyone greeted each other with those "Oh, so good to see you" kind of "we only see each other at these events" but "we talk often on the phone – it's great to put a face to the name" kind of greetings.

I was like a gooseberry, standing there next to the event organising crew who were trying to work out my place there. Anyway, I mingled awkwardly until the guest speaker took to the stage. I was in awe of Justin's presentation style, story, his connection with the audience.

As soon as he finished, I raced forward with a copy of his book for signing. I seriously was like an obsessed groupie. He chatted and signed the book. He remembered me!

So, now I knew I needed some tips from an accomplished adventurer. I called. He answered. I told him of my state of mind, shared my fears of being so close, yet so far from the start line. I rattled off my enormous last-minute to-do list and finally took a breath, to wait for him to respond.

He completely changed my world with words of wisdom that calmed and set me straight.

He said: "Michelle, make 2 lists. On one, list all of your wishes, wants – perfect world, no expense spared items and then make another list, this time only put the lifesaving, absolute essential, non-negotiable items. Now throw away the first list and just focus on the second list."

Keeping lists was something I got used to and relied on during my preparation. I had a white board at home that I would dump things on in the middle of the night if I woke up with things on my mind.

I heard that if you can "dump" the thoughts, you would be able to go straight back to sleep. It is true. It worked a treat, except that sometimes I couldn't read what I had scribbled!

Back to Jonesy. As he laughed light heartedly, he completed his sentence with "because you will never get to the end of the perfect world list. Well, blow me away. How sensible is that and all of a sudden, the overwhelm disappeared and was replaced with "this is actually achievable now."

Change your perspective and you change your attitude. Put a fresh head on.

This was actually something that came to me, in the middle of hissy fit number 148. It was a moment when I was actually slamming my equipment around with total disrespect and regard. I was not getting my way and mother nature was teaching me a lesson. I was in the height of my moment, embarrassing if anyone could see it.

Through gritted teeth I was slamming my oars in the rowlock and bashing them around like a brat chucking a huge tantrum. Not only does it exert a shit load of precious energy, it raises blood pressure, increases cortisol levels and removes the capability to apply reason and logic to the situation at hand.

My behaviour could have broken my rowlock. the gate that houses my oar shaft. The instant I realised that, I quickly let go of the oar and began apologising out loud, to my boat, for being so disrespectful and rough. I asked for forgiveness. I cried. I never lost my shit again in temper. Treat your equipment well and it will look after you.

After that incident I found myself talking to my auto pilot – even named her "my Angel." I used to tell her, "We'll get through this to the end, together." From that moment on I would nurse her – my angel. I would adjust my angle to the wind to keep her happy and avoid labouring her little motor.

Conditions for a happy auto pilot require you to be running with the conditions or at least to be doing 7 knots or above. I sat on 2 – 3 knots and often was not blessed with a running sea.

In order to keep my Angel happy, I was often sacrificing the bearing or direction that I really wanted to go. That leads into choosing acceptance over resistance.

But first, one more mention and tribute to the white board. Day 10 of 68 , I questioned my 24-hour rowing mile stats. I was chatting to Tony (my DPA) and he was relaying what the other solo rowers were achieving in miles.

I wondered what on earth was I doing wrong. My numbers were significant lower.

Then it dawned on me. Discipline! I was lacking discipline. So – out comes the white board.

Yes. I had a whiteboard on my boat. Now it just got some

purpose. Logging my rowing shifts with start time, latitude / longitude, bearing. I would set a timer and not get out of that rowing seat until the bell went, 90 mins later.

If I felt good, I would set it for another 90 minutes. My ability to row for three hours was dependant on my state of hunger. As you get depleted or hungry, you start to lose coordination and feel generally silly in the head.

This is when I knew that I had to refuel.

CHAPTER 18

THE MARKETING NIGHTMARE

PERSISTENCE PAYS OFF

Don't let perfection get in the way of progress – this advice goes along way.

We can easily give up on a project or idea when something goes a little less to plan than the scenario we had in our heads.

The process of goal-setting requires flexibility and preparedness to cop some letdowns, unexpected mishaps and sometimes truly disastrous hiccups.

Tony used to say, "It's just one more splinter in your arse as you slide down the banister of life." In other words, no matter what, the show goes on.

Frustration can be the dominating emotion when a less-than-perfect world interrupts the carefully thought out, perfect-on-paper, this-is-what-should-happen plans. Take for example my fundraising campaign.

With all my target and potential sponsors lined up, hours of thought were spent pouring over each one.

With the benefits, ROI, alignment warm and fuzzies set out I thought I had the cat in bag. I could have sworn that I would have them begging for a space on my boat with their logo on display, for a price of course.

I learned my first lesson in marketing.

Here I am, armed with the perfect elevator pitch, the 60-second spiel meant to have the listener wanting more. Imagine delivering it as the elevator door is sliding shut. Boom. Just as you manage to rattle off only just enough to leave them curious to hear more: "I am preparing to row solo across the Atlantic Ocean. I will become Australia's first woman on the world to row any ocean, ssolo, alone, non-stop and unassisted..."

Hmm. That was all I had. I used almost to mumble it. There was a level of embarrassment of bragging about something that I didn't even know whether I could do it. I found it difficult to own. I had no runs on the board – so to speak. You know – credentials or validating records. So, I was trying to convince people to back me, when I was struggling to back myself.

Then, I had to sell this: Salt sores, blisters, capsizing, system failures, mental fatigue, physical exhaustion, foot waves. Yeah. Wanna row an ocean with me. Would you like to sponsor me?

Then they would ask "Oh, so you're a rower?" – No

"Oh – well you're elite, an athlete?" – No

"Oh – but you have a boat?" No

See. This was a marketing nightmare and the fact that I had no credibility or impressive flag to fly, I must have appeared just plain mad. Plus, I had to deliver all of this as though it was irrelevant that my CV did not warrant support.

This was a tougher gig than I imagined it could be. The Million-meter world record row proved to be the perfect ingredient. At least then I would have some of title, it was relevant and it would serve as the credibility and validation. It gave me that all important "run on the board."

I also built my confidence in myself, making it easier to actually" back myself". The value of earning your place on stage was highlighted in this achievement.

Don't forget, I also learnt how to row, the importance of nutrition and an even more valuable lesson: what worked "for me". I had time to practice, trial and note the things that served me well, or hindered my digestion.

So the things I can attest to from my on-the-job, untrained, naïve and thrown-in-the-deep-end marketing experience is that;
a) You have to be able to walk the walk to truly talk the talk;
b) Do the work – earn your place on the podium. The sell is much easier and you can be more convincing, confident and worth it;
c) Have broad shoulders. Be able to withstand the knockbacks and rejection – because it is inevitable.
d) Go to the top. This saves time, the closer you can get to the decision maker, the better the outcome.

• • •

My Hyundai sponsor came at the end of a day in which I had literally walked the whole street of 10 car dealerships. I walked in and out of each one, delivering my elevator pitch to the young girl sitting behind the desk of the big fancy show room.

I think it is a pre requisite that the pretty young woman must have eyelashes that look like she might just fly away as she bats them in front of you. Oh, and they must be young and gorgeous. My challenge was to get past her. More difficult than my skill set possessed.

They were less than impressed, didn't care or both, and very assertively told me to "send an email".

I just wanted to talk the manager. He was sitting right there, in the glass office behind the gatekeeper. He could hear me. Wow. That was a shock and a revelation that no one wanted to do face-to-face communication anymore.

I walked on, door-knocking persistently and treating each one as though it was my first and as if they **were** going to love the idea and eagerly usher me in to sit down, while I sold them the package.

Of course, it was not that easy and people were not that inviting. Then, on my last door to knock on, after being rejected too many times than is good for the ego, BINGO.

Hyundai. Finally, the gorgeous young lady asked if I wanted to chat to the sales manager. Wow. Yes please.

I sat in front of Guy and told him of my plans to become Australia's first woman to row across any ocean solo and he asked straight to the point, no mucking around, "What do you need? What can Hyundai do to help?" He just got it.

I said, "I need a car, to tow that boat around Sydney to different venues, boat ramps, up to Queensland to boat shows." He said, "Leave it with me."

Just two days later I had to go and pick up the most amazing, top of the line, all the bells and whistles, Hyundai Santa Fe. I could not believe it.

The moral of this is to neve take no for an answer, apply persistence and consistency to the project and keep the end result (objective) clear, in your mind. This sets a new vibrational frequency in which you will operate from and attract the wavelength and people on it – to your desired channel (outcome).

I experienced many of these miracle-like responses.

CHAPTER 19

QUANTUM PHYSICS

You need persistence. If I had of given up and not continued, the wave, signal or energy into the universe would not have connected.

The idea of "you get what you think about, even if you don't want it" is true, 100 percent.

It has proven itself over and over. The story about the Hyundai is classic example. All the door knocking was the seed being planted, the frequency was being set and to know that this takes some incubation time, you will find the persistence part, easier.

Every thought carries an energy. Words have energy. "You reap what you sow" is also an example of the practical meaning. In the words of Dr Joe Dispenza, "Life is about the management of energy. Wherever you place your attention, is where you place your energy".

Consider replacing your screen time, whether that be FB, TV or gaming. How many frivolous mind-numbing hours would that equate to? What skill set could you learn or master if you applied that conscious, focused attention to one thing?

I can speak from experience, with my self-obsessed, self-taught ukelele talent.

I was inspired by Josh Kaufmann. He did a TED talk on the benefits of applying 20 hours of fairdinkum conscious, focused attention to one thing. I did this with my roomie. We both went out and purchased a cheap uke from Carlingford music shop.

Neither of us had any idea and had no strumming or chord changing experience at all. Through watching, copying and mimicking the YouTube clips, we mastered the four chords required to play more than 100 songs!

It was the coolest thing to see develop before our own eyes. We went from single down strums to up, up, down , up to down, down, up, up, down, up. Our chords increased and so did our repertoire (song list). We even mastered the singing and playing combo; it took longer than the 20 hours but with perseverance, we did it.

The unnatural nature of hands doing complex activity and then getting the brain to operate the mouth and make words come out, from memory, was not pretty at first.

The brain is fascinating and marvellous. Being able to actually sing and strum and maintain the rhythm and beat took way more than the suggested 20 hours as suggested by Josh. But, we got there!

I completely bought the idea and so my sub conscious mind was already on an accelerated learning growth path.

The saying, "If you believe you can't, you won't" is as true as "believe you can, and you will" The power of the mind is not to be underestimated and then when you add faith to your gut feeling – your instincts – that kne- jerk reaction kind of feeling, you are now unstoppable. It is all energy.

The vibration of the energy that you project can have a positive or negative effect on the people around you. Knowing this, you would know then, that you can manifest outcomes. You have the power within you to create a whole new reality.

How about the idea of your thoughts can make you sick? That is said as in a statement. Can you use your thoughts then, to make yourself well? Yes! You can. How exciting is this fact?

By becoming more aware and conscious to your spoken words, you can change the present situation.

My friend Jacinta was walking around saying, "I am sick of hearing it!". She would use this statement often during the height of the pandemic. Next thing, she had an earache. Jacinta has done a lot of personal growth over a four-year period and one of the courses she completed was the Jose Silva "Ultra mind method."

After suffering for a few days she caught herself, mid-sentence. Oh my god, she said, "Listen to myself – I am walking around repeating 'I am sick of hearing it'. Once she acknowledged this and consciously changed her language, the earache stopped!

This story is one of many I could share to explain the power of words. The other fact to note is that they don't even have to be spoken. They can be thoughts. So, to be fully aware of what you are thinking and how you are acting will bring change to the outcome that you desire.

. . .

Thoughts and energy you project determine the vibration and frequency you attract. I love the teachings from Dr Joe Dispenza, Dr Bruce Lipton and Gregg Braden.

They are the pioneers in this field in modern day times. They hold seminars and workshops on how to master the power of the mind.

My tool kit has a combination of these techniques as well as my recent guru/go-to Jose Silva-method. If you can control your mind, regardless of the situational circumstances, you can overcome, triumph and shine in all conditions.

The ability to "put on a fresh head" and see another perspective will change your attitude and ultimately it will change your outcome. It is a discipline that has to be practiced.

I think of it like a muscle; to strengthen, build and grow, you must apply a stimulus. Then, in time, new habits are formed and it becomes second nature.

I am not going to say that I never slip up or fall from grace, but, the awareness brings me back on track sooner and I spend less time in the less conscious zone.

I love my new challenge to stay on track. This awareness will get better in time and my struggles will become less. I think struggle is indicative of how "out of alignment" with source you are. When I say source, I am referring to the divine, guidance, right path, your calling – you know what I mean.

The idea that we can control a situation with proper mind control is pretty damn exciting, just like we can change the way our genes are acting with the understanding that epi genetics is a reflection of the way genes are responding to the environment being created.

Once you understand, know and trust this theory, you can begin immediately to change the way your genes express themselves. Again, this takes discipline, belief and expectancy. You must apply the positive thoughts, visions, desires as though they have already happened. This means that you are now acting from a place of gratitude and abundance.

The other great news is – that anyone can do it. Get in touch with your intuition, respect and honour it and you will be well on your way to witnessing a change in your life and how the people respond to you. This can then also be your meter; look at your results and be prepared to change your energy, vibration, approach or strategy for a better outcome.

The thing to note is that you will not get it right 100 per cent of the time but the more you practice, the less time you will spend in the negatively charged zone. I also love knowing the fact that your sub conscious believes what you tell it, taking it literally. Once you are aware of this and can put points of reference to the theory – I mean, times when it has displayed what I am talking about- you can then change your words, add desire, belief and expectancy. The winds will change, in your favour. Become more learned with these techniques by following Dr Joe Dispenza, Gregg Braden and Dr Bruce Lipton. Others in this quantum physics field include Abraham Hicks.

I also love Louise Hayes – Heal yourself. She explains disease in the body as the manifestations of our reactions to our external environment.

I know it to be true and can relate personally with my lifetime of severe sufferings with dermatitis and eczema.

As a child, from as long as I can remember, my skin was red, inflamed, itchy, broken and sore. The pain was intense as I would scratch myself raw, until I bled. Mum would stand me on the kitchen table nightly and wrap my limbs in plastic glad wrap – smeared with a thick greasy ointment.

I was a long-time user of topical cortisone and anti-histamines. As a child I knew that I could manipulate my parents during a raging argument. So, it served a purpose, to a certain degree.

I recognise it now. My skin would flare up in times of turmoil and unrest between Mum and Dad. If there was that negative, aggressive or abusive energy at home, my skin would flare up, I would then be in distress and crying which would inevitably create a distraction and I would eventually have to be attended to.

See, the diversion killed the arguing in that instance. It was a pattern. As I matured and found myself on a path that sought out truth, I found the answer to breaking that patter. It took work. Lots of practice.

I got trained by a professional EFT practitioner. Molly Knight, my naturopath. She taught me and wrote my first few initial scripts to follow, until I got in the groove.

There is a massive level of intuition that helps your practitioner

– if you get the real deal (a good one). They will encourage you to come up with your own.

It has been amazing in my life. I still use it. The tapping is an interruption to the effects of the emotion, when applied to specific points along the meridians of the body. There are about seven sites that you tap on, whilst saying the emotion you feel when...(insert the stressor or trigger).

I used it on my boat when I had to go overboard. I was sitting there, suffering a case of the "Oh, no, I can't do this." I had fears of a shark being under the boat, just waiting for me to get in the water.

After wasting 10 minutes or more, I decided to do a round of tapping. In three minutes, I tested the emotion. It was gone! No fear.

I laughed at myself for being so ridiculous and jumped over the side to get under my boat and scrape the bottom of the hull. How easy was that!

Seriously, find a practitioner and overcome the fears that paralyse you or stop you from soaring above the skies like an eagle. Snakes, spiders, fear of heights, illness, anxiety, they are all treatable with notable results when you practice. If it does not work the first time, keep at it. It is new to your body and paradigm, so, give it a good chance.

· · ·

I want to mention more about "point of reference". This is so important because it is what will build your confidence to trust your intuition.

Every time you have one of those moments where you say either, "Wow, I knew I should have done (insert here)" or vice versa, "I knew I shouldn't have gone..." (insert appropriately a time when you went against your better judgement for whatever reason).

Then, focus on the times you acted in alignment with your gut and you achieved the outcome that was best for you. This is a positive point of reference. Now, let this confidence serve you. Remember you don't have to even understand why you may have an inclination or a stance on something, at the time. It usually reveals itself and you find yourself having an "Ah Ha" moment. Again – that's a point of reference to lock in.

I had it so strongly with jabs. I knew it wasn't right – FOR ME!

So, I stood strong in my convictions and refused to fall into line. The bullying, coercion, manipulation and lack of transparency sent violent vibrations of resistance through my body. My gut screamed no. So, can you see the violation and betrayal that I would have suffered, if I went against it?

This would not have given a positive point of reference. There would have been feelings of remorse, resentment, betrayal and guilt. They are all extremely low vibrations. It is essential that you trust your instincts. I cannot harp on this enough. Read and listen to the teachings of Dispenza, Lipton and Gregg Bradden. Once you connect to the quantum field of energy it will be easy. Like anything – once you know, it is easy.

• • •

Another true story of the law of attraction, my most recent: I was sitting on my boat, on the trailer, in the boat ramp at Cammeray.

A gentleman named Colin came and introduced himself to me and was interested in learning the whereabouts of my next journey. He said he had followed my last journey.

When he learned that I had to depart from West Coast USA, he asked if I needed a marina to help me out at the start line. "Why, yes I do," I replied. He just happened to be the retired CEO of the Marina Industry Association. And, he knew the CEO of the MIA, on the west coast.

How is that for that for a meaningful coincidence. I have many of those stories. I know it, without question, that when you are operating from a vibration of truth, with your conscious intention at the core of your actions, you will attract more of this into your life.

When these incidents stop happening in my life, I actually ask myself, "What am I doing wrong?" Usually I have gone off the path of direct alignment with what my goal or objective is at that time. This is also why consistency and persistence pay off.

It is much easier to keep an energy vibrating than let it stop completely and then try to come to pick up where you left off.

Momentum is easy to keep going; the work and effort is in the building phase – the thought or conception phase. We all want everything right now. That does not help the process. Trust that your efforts in the warming, moulding, introducing moments of the idea are the seeds being planted. Then, the connections and the progress through consistent steps are the doors that open and the way things appear as you need them.

Being in alignment with yourself can also bring healing to ailments or your pre disposed illnesses.

I look at my skin flare ups as the perfect example. I know I used it in my childhood to stop an argument between Mum and Dad, or to get what I wanted from time to time.

I have witnessed the exchange of energy often between my flat-mate and her poodle. They have such a strong bond and emotional connection that one suffers the same gut upsets as the other, in sync! It is undeniable.

You have heard about sympathy pains. This also is a transference of energy between two people who are in alignment or connected spiritually or emotionally.

I am looking forward to learning the art of mental telepathy before I embark on my Pacific Ocean row. I have my person in mind. In fact I know exactly who that will be. It is Jacinta. She did the Jose Silva course with me and has been practicing raising her spiritual being for some time now. She already has an intuitive side that resonates with me. There are techniques you can apply and with practice, perfect. So in the event that I possibly lose all sat comms, Jacinta and I will be able to communicate using telepathy. It happens often.

You will be familiar with those moments when the phone rings and it is the very person that you had on your mind. You more than likely even answer the phone with, "Oh my god, I was just going to call you!" This is mental telepathy.

Thoughts travel through space and time. It is a frequency that you can reach and become good at it. I had my osteo, Julian Howard, do a healing session on me. It was remote, meaning that at 8pm, I had to sit quietly, undistracted and be ready and open to receive a healing through Julian's conscious and focused intention.

Later, he said my chakras were spinning wildly. Well, the other side of that story is that as I sat, ready to receive, I was practicing an awakening of the chakras, by Dr Joe Dispenza.

It is a meditation technique that I had never tried before. Lo and behold, Julian could sense or feel or see, my chakras spinning wildly.

I relayed that info to him so that it could become a positive point of reference for him, so that he knew whatever he did during that healing, was right. Spot on, in fact!

Julian would then put that in his conscious mind and it will sit in the sub conscious. You can help anyone with your thoughts and by using light. Bright white light is a powerful technique that we can use to heal any ailment. I completely healed my torn elbow tendon. Three times a day, for 15 minutes each.

I would lie down and do a 17-minute guided mediation with Jose Silva. This would get me in the alpha state and then I would finish with images of bright white light enveloping my elbow, Then, I would use my imagination to create a laser light, in the palm of my hand and I would aim it the tear and damaged elbow.

Also, I was advised by Jeanine, a Jose Silva instructor, to get creative and have an army or something inside my elbow, making the repairs. For this I imagined a little granny, lovingly darning my tears back together.

It was a beautiful thing to do and I felt as if I was taking control of my healing. providing the tools for my body to heal quicker. In record time, I was released from the physio. Again, this is a super powerful positive point of reference.

Once you know that you can do something, it is easy to replicate and duplicate. The believer is even more powerful. You can do it more efficiently the more you practice it.

The important thing to know is that it requires diligence and discipline. Like anything. Remember, Dr Joe says where you place your attention, you place your energy. We can heal ourselves. Our bodies just need the nurturing environment, awareness and gratitude. Say thank you. Acknowledge the greatness within you. Explore and play with these possibilities, often.

You will be amazed at the change you can create, without side effects, without contra-indications and without delay. Start now. Today. Invest in you. It doesn't even cost anything.

CHAPTER 20

LAND HO

There were days I didn't think I was ever going to get there.

You are just so tired ... there's no tired like it.

I had never gone through so many emotions in my life. Isolation, being overwhelmed, there was joy, I was in awe of so many things. I was anxious, nervous.

I had to deal with strong tides, storms, broken equipment, health issues, injury and wildlife.

There were holes in my fingers from gripping the oars and massive callouses on my hands. I had sores on my bottom as well from 12 hours in the seat. I had toothaches and earaches, which I managed to fix with a bit of self-help — three courses of antibiotics. All of it made me realise how vulnerable I was.

I cut my hand, had diarrhoea and had to dive under the boat to clean off pipis that had attached themselves and made rowing harder.

It was terribly confronting and frightening at times.

Quite often I felt Mother Nature was working against me.

The wildlife - there were dolphins. I had full-on dolphin armies with me, and whale armies come through. The bird life was unbelievable every day.

Determination, grit and integrity. Integrity for me is to finish what you start and to do what you'll say you'll do. They're the big things for me.

We are so much more capable of what we think we are. When you think there's nothing left in the tank, there is shedloads.

Start thinking you can, and you will. It's that simple. That's what all this started from.

...

On Day 35 in my row across the I was deciding what to have for dinner. I thought, "What would I do if I rowed the Pacific. The seed was sown.

It's a nine to 12 month journey. I think it would be so cool to roll into Australian shores and inspire a nation. My motto is 'start thinking you can and you will' so it would be great to show Aussies what we can do.

I feel like I need to recreate something as my normal isn't appealing anymore – I feel like I'm walking around in circles and not really achieving anything.

The preparations will be mighty and so will be the challenges.

I made a lot of mistakes during my Atlantic row, just because there were so many things I couldn't have possibly known until I did it, so I feel compelled to do one more ocean row.

My essentials are a packet of photos of the people who mean the most to me, Nutella (don't run out), enough podcasts and books; just lots more learning material and educational kind of books.

I also have a go-to box, my routine and ritual box. Moisturise, cleanse, take my homeopathic kit. It's something that you stick to and it's grounding. Having a routine is very important.

I start every single rowing with the Queen album, I don't know why, I don't even like them that much but I do.

I was lacking in Oxytocin, the love drug the last time. Oxytocin includes physically touching and feeling like stroking a pet or even just being in service to someone.

This was what I was lacking in my last row. So this time, I'm taking two teddy bears with me to hug.

I also learned to hug myself; literally wrap your arms around myself. It's important to visualise and imagine this for the oxytocin to flow. These were things I didn't even think about last time, but they're so important and are enough to top up that hormone.

It's a hack. You can hack your feel-good hormone by the lifestyle you choose: sunshine, tick; nature, tick; feeling the love, tick.

Will this see me safely across the Pacific? That's another story.